Workshop on GEometrical Models of Natural Language Semantics 2011

(GEMS 2011)

Held at EMNLP 2011

Edinburgh, Scotland, UK
31 July 2011

ISBN: 978-1-61839-237-4

Printed from e-media with permission by:

Curran Associates, Inc.
57 Morehouse Lane
Red Hook, NY 12571

Some format issues inherent in the e-media version may also appear in this print version.

Printed by Curran Associates, Inc. (2011)

For permission requests, please contact the Association for Computational Linguistics at the address below.

Association for Computational Linguistics
209 N. Eighth Street
Stroudsburg, Pennsylvania 18360

Phone: 1-570-476-8006
Fax: 1-570-476-0860

acl@aclweb.org

Additional copies of this publication are available from:

Curran Associates, Inc.
57 Morehouse Lane
Red Hook, NY 12571 USA
Phone: 845-758-0400
Fax: 845-758-2634
Email: curran@proceedings.com
Web: www.proceedings.com

Introduction

GEMS 2011 — GEometrical Models of Natural Language Semantics — is the third instalment in a successful series of workshops on distributional models of meaning. Since their earliest application in information retrieval, these models have become omnipresent in contemporary computational linguistics and neighboring fields. Different types of distributional models have been introduced — from the relatively simple bag-of-word, document-based and syntax-based techniques to the statistically more advanced topic models. In the field of lexical semantics, their direct applications include the construction of lexical taxonomies, the recognition of textual entailment, word sense discrimination and disambiguation, cognitive modeling, etc. Moreover, other areas of NLP, like parsing and Machine Translation, have found they can indirectly benefit from the ability of distributional models to generalize from a limited training set to unseen, but semantically similar, words.

The growth of distributional semantics, however, is not without its problems. The aim of GEMS is to address two orthogonal types of current challenges. First, there is the fragmentation with regard to data sets, methods and evaluation metrics, which makes it difficult to compare studies and achieve scientific progress. We addressed this problem by providing authors with two datasets suitable for the evaluation of distributional models, together with the corpora that can be used for their construction. As a result, the performance of very different approaches can be easily compared across papers. Second, these datasets were chosen so as to reflect two of the most pressing issues in the development of distributional models nowadays: differentiation between semantic relations and compositionality.

The first set, presented by Baroni and Lenci, includes concrete nouns from different semantic classes (living, non-living, etc.) with associated words for specific semantic relations such as "attribute", "category coordinate", "event", or "metonym". Panchenko uses this data to compare 21 measures of semantic similarity and relatedness, based on information from WordNet, a traditional corpus, and the web. Baroni, Bruni and Binh Tran explore images as a fourth type of information. Both papers discover fundamental differences in the semantic information that is captured by these different sources of information. This paves the way for a combined, more comprehensive model.

The second dataset, borrowed from Mitchell and Lapata, contains phrase similarity judgments. It makes it possible to address the evaluation of distributional models in compositional tasks. Grefenstette and Sadrzadeh show how a transitive verb can be modeled as a matrix and combine with the vectors of its subject and object. Basile, Caputo and Semeraro use vector permutation in a Random Indexing framework to encode different syntactic dependency relations. Hartung and Frank look to Latent Dirichlet Allocation to identify the dimensions of meaning modified by adjectives.

In addition, the workshop was open to any other original application of distributional semantics. Chan, Callison-Burch and Van Durme use distributional similarity to evaluate paraphrases extracted from a bilingual lexicon. Gulordava and Baroni investigate meaning change in the Google Books corpus.

Obviously, the success of a workshop does not only rely on the quality of its papers. In addition to all speakers and participants, we would like to thank the members of the organizing committee and program committee, who where indispensable for the preparation of the workshop. We also thank our panelists and invited speaker for their thought-provoking contributions, and the ACL SIGSEM and ACL SIGLEX interest groups for their endorsement of the workshop.

Chairs:

Sebastian Padó, University of Heidelberg
Yves Peirsman, University of Leuven & Stanford University

Organizing Committee:

Marco Baroni, University of Trento
Alessandro Lenci, University of Pisa

Program Committee:

Enrique Alfonseca, Google Research
Roberto Basili, University of Roma Tor Vergata
Michael W. Berry, University of Tennessee
Johan Bos, University of Roma La Sapienza
Paul Buitelaar, National University of Ireland
John A. Bullinaria, University of Birmingham
Stefan Evert, University of Osnabrueck
Gregory Grefenstette, Exalead S.A.
Emiliano Guevara, University of Bologna
Matthias Hartung, University of Heidelberg
Iris Hendrickx, University of Lisbon
Kris Heylen, University of Leuven
Jussi Karlgren, Swedish Institute of Computer Science
Zornitsa Kozareva, University of Southern California
Will Lowe, University of Mannheim
Diana McCarthy, Lexical Computing Ltd.
Lukas Michelbacher, University of Stuttgart
Saif Mohammad, University of Maryland
Alessandro Moschitti, University of Trento
Diarmuid O Seaghdha, Cambridge University
Ted Pedersen, University of Minnesota Duluth
Marco Pennacchiotti, Yahoo! Inc.
Daniel Ramage, Stanford University
Lorenza Romano, Fondazione Bruno Kessler
Magnus Sahlgren, Swedish Institute of Computer Science
Sabine Schulte im Walde, University of Stuttgart
Stefan Thater, Saarland University
Peter D. Turney, National Research Council of Canada & University of Ottawa
Tim Van de Cruys, Cambridge University
Yorick Wilks, University of Sheffield
Fabio Massimo Zanzotto, University of Roma Tor Vergata

Invited Speaker:

Mirella Lapata, University of Edinburgh

Panelists:

Roberto Basili & Danilo Croce, University of Roma Tor Vergata
Mona Diab, Columbia University
Annette Frank, University of Heidelberg
Alessandro Lenci, University of Pisa
Peter Turney, National Research Council of Canada & University of Ottawa

Table of Contents

Workshop Program

Sunday, July 31, 2011

8:50–9:00 Opening remarks

9:00–10:00 Invited talk by Mirella Lapata: "Distributional Models of the Representation and Acquisition of Natural Language Categories"

10:00–10:30 *How we BLESSed distributional semantic evaluation*
Marco Baroni and Alessandro Lenci

10:30–11:00 Coffee break

11:00–11:30 *Comparison of the Baseline Knowledge-, Corpus-, and Web-based Similarity Measures for Semantic Relations Extraction*
Alexander Panchenko

11:30–12:00 *Distributional semantics from text and images*
Elia Bruni, Giang Binh Tran and Marco Baroni

12:00–12:30 *Reranking Bilingually Extracted Paraphrases Using Monolingual Distributional Similarity*
Tsz Ping Chan, Chris Callison-Burch and Benjamin Van Durme

12:30–14:00 Lunch

14:00–14:30 *Encoding syntactic dependencies by vector permutation*
Pierpaolo Basile, Annalina Caputo and Giovanni Semeraro

14:30–15:00 *Assessing Interpretable, Attribute-related Meaning Representations for Adjective-Noun Phrases in a Similarity Prediction Task*
Matthias Hartung and Anette Frank

15:00–15:20 *Experimenting with transitive verbs in a DisCoCat*
Edward Grefenstette and Mehrnoosh Sadrzadeh

15:20–15:40 *A distributional similarity approach to the detection of semantic change in the Google Books Ngram corpus.*
Kristina Gulordava and Marco Baroni

15:40–16:10 Coffee break

Sunday, July 31, 2011 (continued)

16:10–17:30 Closing session

Invited talk by Peter Turney: "GEMS as the Missing Link between Computational Linguistics and Cognitive Linguistics"

Invited talk by Roberto Basili and Danilo Croce: "Distributional Information, Syntactic Kernels and Compositionality"

Panel discussion

How we BLESSed distributional semantic evaluation

Marco Baroni
University of Trento
Trento, Italy
marco.baroni@unitn.it

Alessandro Lenci
University of Pisa
Pisa, Italy
alessandro.lenci@ling.unipi.it

Abstract

We introduce BLESS, a data set specifically designed for the evaluation of distributional semantic models. BLESS contains a set of tuples instantiating different, explicitly typed semantic relations, plus a number of controlled random tuples. It is thus possible to assess the ability of a model to detect truly related word pairs, as well as to perform in-depth analyses of the types of semantic relations that a model favors. We discuss the motivations for BLESS, describe its construction and structure, and present examples of its usage in the evaluation of distributional semantic models.

1 Introduction

In NLP, it is customary to distinguish between *intrinsic evaluations*, testing a system in itself, and *extrinsic evaluations*, measuring its performance in some task or application (Sparck Jones and Galliers, 1996). For instance, the intrinsic evaluation of a dependency parser will measure its accuracy in identifying specific syntactic relations, while its extrinsic evaluation will focus on the impact of the parser on tasks such as question answering or machine translation. Current approaches to the evaluation of **Distributional Semantic Models** (DSMs, also known as semantic spaces, vector-space models, etc.; see Turney and Pantel (2010) for a survey) are task-oriented. Model performance is evaluated in "semantic tasks", such as detecting synonyms, recognizing analogies, modeling verb selectional preferences, ranking paraphrases, etc. Measuring the performance of DSMs on such tasks represents an *indirect test* of their ability to capture lexical meaning. The task-oriented benchmarks adopted in distributional semantics have not specifically been designed to evaluate DSMs. For instance, the widely used TOEFL synonym detection task was designed to test the learners' proficiency in English as a second language, and not to investigate the structure of their semantic representations (cf. Section 2).

To gain a real insight into the abilities of DSMs to address lexical semantics, existing benchmarks must be complemented with a more intrinsically oriented approach, to perform *direct tests* on the specific aspects of lexical knowledge captured by the models. In order to achieve this goal, three conditions must be met: (i) to single out the particular aspects of meaning that we want to focus on in the evaluation of DSMs; (ii) to design a data set that is able to explicitly and reliably encode the target semantic information; (iii) to specify the evaluation criteria of the system performance on the data set, in order to get an estimate of the intrinsic ability of DSMs to cope with the selected semantic aspects. In this paper, we address these three conditions by presenting **BLESS** (**B**aroni and **L**enci **E**valuation of **S**emantic **S**paces), a new data set specifically geared towards the intrinsic evaluation of DSMs, downloadable from: http://clic.cimec.unitn.it/distsem.

2 Distributional semantics benchmarks

There are several benchmarks that have been widely adopted for the evaluation of DSMs, all of them capturing interesting challenges a DSM should meet. We briefly review here some commonly used and representative benchmarks, and discuss why we felt the need to add BLESS to the set. We notice at the outset of this discussion that we want to carve out a space for BLESS, and not to detract from the importance and usefulness of other data sets. We further remark that we focus on data sets that, like BLESS, are monolingual English and, while task-oriented, not aimed at a specific application setting (such as machine translation or ontology population).

Probably the most commonly used benchmark in distributional semantics is the TOEFL **synonym detection task** introduced to computational linguistics by Landauer and Dumais (1997). It consists of 80 multiple-choice questions, each made of a target word (a noun, verb, adjective or adverb) and 4 response words, 1 of them a synonym of the target. For example, given the target *levied*, the matched words are *imposed*, *believed*, *requested*, *correlated*, the first one being the correct choice. The task for a system is then to pick the true synonym among the responses. The TOEFL task focuses on a single semantic relation, namely synonymy. Synonymy is actually not a common semantic relation and one of the hardest to define, to the point that many lexical semanticists have concluded that true synonymy does not exist (Cruse, 1986). Just looking at a few examples of synonym pairs from the TOEFL set will illustrate the problem: *discrepancy/difference*, *prolific/productive*, *percentage/proportion*, *to market/to sell*, *color/hue*. Moreover, the criteria adopted to choose the distractors (probably motivated by the language proficiency testing purposes of TOEFL) are not known. By looking at the set, it is hard to discern a coherent pattern. In certain cases, the distractors are semantically close to the target word (*volume*, *sample* and *profit* for *percentage*), whereas in other cases they are not (*home*, *trail*, and *song* for *annals*). It it thus not clear whether we are asking the models to distinguish a semantically related word (the synonym) from random elements, or a more tightly related word (the synonym, again) from other related words. The TOEFL task, finally, is based on a discrete choice (either you get the right word, or you don't), with the result that evaluation is "quantized", leading to large accuracy gains for small actual differences (one model that guesses one more synonym right than another gets 1.25% more points in percentage accuracy).

The WordSim 353 data set (Finkelstein et al., 2002) is a widely used example of **semantic similarity rating** set (see also Rubenstein and Goodenough (1965) and Miller and Charles (1991)). Subjects were asked to rate a set of 353 word pairs on a "similarity" scale and average ratings for each pair were computed. Models are then evaluated in terms of correlation of their similarity scores with average ratings across pairs. From the point of view of assessing the performance of a DSM, the WordSim (and related) similarity ratings are a mixed bag, in two senses. First, the data set contains a variety of different semantic relations. In a recent semantic annotation of the WordSim performed by Agirre et al. (2009) we find that, among the 174 pairs with above-median score (and thus presumably related), there is 1 identical pair, 17 synonym pairs, 28 hyper-/hyponym pairs, 30 coordinate pairs, 6 holo-/meronym pairs and 92 (more than half) pairs that are "topically related, but none of the above". Second, the scores are a mixture of intuitions about which of these relations are more semantically tight and intuitions about more or less connected pairs *within* each of the relations. For example, among the top-rated scores we find synonyms such as *journey/voyage* and coordinate concepts (*king/queen*). If we look at the relations characterizing pairs around the median rating, we find both less "perfect" synonyms (*monk/brother*, that are synonymous only under an unusual sense of *brother*) and less close coordinates (*skin/eye*), as well as pairs instantiating other, less taxonomically tight relations, such as many syntagmatically connected items (*family/planning*, *disaster/area*, *bread/butter*). Apparently, a single scale is merging intuitions about semantic similarity of specific pairs and semantic similarity of different relations.

A perhaps more principled way to evaluate DSMs that has recently gained some popularity is the **concept categorization task**, where a DSM has to cluster a set of nouns expressing basic-level concepts into gold standard categories. A particularly carefully constructed example is the Almuhareb-Poesio (AP) set of 402 concepts introduced in Almuhareb (2006). Concept categorization sets also include the Battig (Baroni et al., 2010) and ESSLLI 2008 (Baroni et al., 2008) lists. The AP concepts must be clustered into 21 classes, each represented by between 13 and 21 nouns. Examples include the *ve-*

hicle class (*helicopter*, *motorcycle*...), the *motivation* class (*ethics*, *incitement*, ...), and the *social unit* class (*platoon*, *branch*). The concepts are balanced in terms of frequency and ambiguity, so that, e.g., the *tree* class contains a common concept such as *pine* but also the *casuarina* tree, as well as the *samba* tree, that is not only an ambiguous term, but one where the non-arboreal sense dominates.

Concept categorization data sets, while interesting to simulate one of the basic aspects of human cognition, are limited to one kind of semantic relation (discovering coordinates). More importantly, the quality of the results will depend not only on the underlying DSMs, but also on the clustering algorithm being used (and on how this interacts with the overall structure of the DSM), thus making it hard to interpret the performance of DSMs. The forced "hard" category choice is also problematic, and exaggerates performance differences between models especially in the presence of ambiguous terms (a model that puts *samba* in the *occasion* class with *dance* and *ball* might be penalized as much as a model that puts it in the *monetary currency* class).

A more general issue with all benchmarks is that tasks are based on comparing a single quality score for each considered model (accuracy for TOEFL, correlation for WordSim, a clustering quality measure for AP, etc.). This gives little insight into *how* and *why* the models differ. Moreover, there is no well-established statistical procedure to assess significance of differences for most commonly used measures. Finally, either because the data sets were not originally intended as standard benchmarks, or even on purpose, they all are likely to cause coverage problems even for DSMs trained on very large corpora. Think of the presence of extremely rare nouns like *casuarina* in AP, of proper nouns in WordSim (it is not clear to us that DSMs are adequate semantic models for referring expressions – at the very least they should not be mixed up lightly with common nouns), or multi-word expressions in other data sets.

3 How we intend to BLESS distributional semantic evaluation

DSMs measure the distributional similarity between words, under the assumption that proximity in distributional space models semantic relatedness, including, as a special case, semantic similarity (Budanitsky and Hirst, 2006). However, semantically related words in turn differ for the type of relation holding between them: e.g., *dog* is strongly related to both *animal* and *tail*, but with different types of relations. Therefore, evaluating the intrinsic ability of DSMs to represent the semantic space of a word entails both (i) determining to what extent words close in semantic space are actually semantically related, and (ii) analyzing, among related words, which type of semantic relation they tend to instantiate. Two models can be equally very good in identifying semantically related words, while greatly differing for the type of related pairs they favor.

The BLESS data set complies with both these constraints. The set is populated with tuples expressing a **relation** between a target concept (henceforth referred to as **concept**) and a relatum concept (henceforth referred to as **relatum**). For instance, in the BLESS tuple *coyote-hyper-animal*, the concept *coyote* is linked to the relatum *animal* via the hypernymy relation (the relatum is a hypernym of the concept). BLESS focuses on a coherent set of basic-level nominal concrete concepts and a small but explicit set of semantic relations, each instantiated by multiple relata. Depending on the type of relation, relata can be nouns, verbs or adjectives. Moreover, BLESS also contains, for each concept, a number of *random* "relatum" words that are not semantically related to the concept. Thus, it also allows to evaluate a model in terms of its ability to harvest related words given a concept (by comparing true and random relata), and to identify specific types of relata, both in terms of semantic relation and part of speech.

A data set intending to represent a gold standard for evaluation should include tests items that are as little controversial as possible. The choice of restricting BLESS to concrete concepts is motivated by the fact that they are by far the most studied ones, and there is better agreement about the relations that characterize them (Murphy, 2002; Rogers and McClelland, 2004).

As for the types of relation to include, we are faced with a dilemma. On the one hand, there is wide evidence that taxonomic relations, the best understood type, only represent a tiny portion of the rich spectrum covered by semantic relatedness. On the other hand, most of these wider semantic relations are also highly controversial, and may easily lead to questionable classifications. For instance, concepts are related to events, but often it is not clear how to distinguish the events expressing a typical function of nominal concepts (e.g., *car* and *transport*), from those events that are also strongly related to them but without representing their typical function *sensu stricto* (e.g., *car* and *fix*). As will be shown in Section 4, the BLESS data set tries to overcome this dilemma by attempting a difficult compromise: Semantic relations are not limited to taxonomic types and also include attributes and events strongly related to a concept, but in these cases we have resorted to underspecification, rather than committing ourselves to questionable granular relations.

BLESS strives to capture those differences and similarities among DSMs that do not depend on coverage, processing choices or lexical preferences. BLESS has been constructed using a publicly available collection of corpora for reference (see Section 4.4 below), which means that anybody can train a DSM on the same data and be sure to have perfect coverage (but this is not strictly necessary). For each concept and relation, we pick a variety of relata (see next section) in order to abstract away from incidental gaps of models or different lexical/topical preferences. For example, the concept *robin* has 7 hypernyms including the very general and non-technical *animal* and *bird* and the more specific and technical *passerine*. A model more geared toward technical terminology might assign a high similarity score to the latter, whereas a commonsense-knowledge-oriented DSM might pick *bird*. Both models have captured similarity with a hypernym, and we have no reason, in general semantic terms, to penalize one or the other. To maximize coverage, we also make sure that, for each concept and relation, a reasonable number of relata are frequently attested in our reference corpora (see statistics below), we only include single-word relata and, where appropriate, we include multiple forms for the same relatum (both *sock* and *socks* as coordinates of *scarf* – as discussed in Section 4.1, we avoided similar ambiguous items as target concepts).

Currently, distributional models for attributional similarity and relational similarity (Turney, 2006) are tested on different data sets, e.g., TOEFL and SAT respectively (briefly, attributional similarity pertains to similarity between a pair of concepts in terms of shared properties, whereas relational similarity measures the similarity of the relations instantiated by couples of concept *pairs*). Conversely, BLESS is not biased towards any particular type of semantic similarity and thus allows both families of models to be evaluated on the same data set. Given a concept, we can analyze the types of relata that are selected by a model as more attributionally similar to the target. Alternatively, given a concept-relatum pair instantiating a specific semantic relation (e.g., hypernymy) we can evaluate a model ability to identify analogically similar pairs, i.e., others concept-relatum pairs instantiating the same relation (we do not illustrate this possibility here).

Finally, by collecting distributions of 200 similarity values for each relation, BLESS allows reliable statistical testing of the significance of differences in similarity within a DSM (for example, using the procedure we present in Section 5 below), as well as across DSMs (for example, via a linear/ANOVA model with relations and DSMs as factors – not illustrated here).

4 Construction

4.1 Concepts

BLESS includes 200 distinct English concrete nouns as target concepts, equally divided between living and non-living entities. Concepts have been grouped into 17 broader classes: AMPHIBIAN_REPTILE (including amphibians and reptiles: *alligator*), APPLIANCE (*toaster*), BIRD (*crow*), BUILDING (*cottage*), CLOTHING (*sweater*), CONTAINER (*bottle*), FRUIT (*banana*), FURNITURE (*chair*), GROUND_MAMMAL (*beaver*), INSECT (*cockroach*), MUSICAL_INSTRUMENT (*violin*), TOOL (i.e., manipulable tools or devices: *hammer*), TREE (*birch*), VEGETABLE (*cabbage*), VEHICLE (*bus*), WATER_ANIMAL (including fish and sea mammals: *herring*), WEAPON (*dagger*).

All 200 BLESS concepts are single-word nouns in the singular form (we avoided concepts such as *socks* whose surface form might change depending on lemmatization choices). The major source we used to select the concepts were the McRae Norms (McRae et al., 2005), a collection of living and non-living basic-level concepts described by 725 subjects with semantic features, each tagged with its property type. As further constraints guiding our selection, we wanted concepts with a reasonably high frequency (cf. Section 4.4), we avoided ambiguous or highly polysemous concepts and we balanced inter- and intra-class composition. Classes include both prototypical and atypical instances (e.g., *robin* and *penguin* for BIRD), and have a wide spectrum of internal variation (e.g., the class VEHICLE contains wheeled, air and sea vehicles). 175 BLESS concepts are attested in the McRae Norms, while the remnants were selected by the authors according to the above constraints. The average number of concepts per class is 11.76 (median 11; min. 5 AMPHIBIAN_REPTILE; max. 21 GROUND_MAMMAL).

4.2 Relations

For each concept noun, BLESS includes several relatum words, linked to the concept by one of the following 5 relations. COORD: the relatum is a noun that is a co-hyponym (coordinate) of the concept, i.e., they belong to the same (narrowly or broadly defined) semantic class: *alligator-coord-lizard*; HYPER: the relatum is a noun that is a hypernym of the concept: *alligator-hyper-animal*; MERO: the relatum is a noun referring to a part/component/organ/member of the concept, or something that the concept contains or is made of: *alligator-mero-mouth*; ATTRI: the relatum is an adjective expressing an attribute of the concept: *alligator-attri-aquatic*; EVENT: the relatum is a verb referring to an action/activity/happening/event the concept is involved in or is performed by/with the concept: *alligator-event-swim*. BLESS also includes the relations RAN.N, RAN.J and RAN.V, which relate the target concepts to control tuples with random noun, adjective and verb relata, respectively.

The BLESS relations cover a wide spectrum of information useful to describe a target concept and to qualify the notion of semantic relatedness: taxonomically related entities (*hyper* and *coord*), typical attributes (*attri*), components (*mero*), and associated events (*event*). However, except for *hyper* and *coord* (corresponding to the standard relations of class inclusion and co-hyponymy respectively), the other BLESS relations are highly underspecified. For instance, *mero* corresponds to a very broad notion of meronymy, including not only parts (*dog-tail*), but also the material (*table-wood*) as well as the members (*hospital-patient*) of the entity the target concept refers to (Winston et al., 1987); *event* is used to represent the behaviors of animals (*dog-bark*), typical functions of instruments (*violin-play*), and events that are simply associated with the target concept (*car-park*); *attri* captures a large range of attributes, from physical (*elephant-big*) to evaluative ones (*car-expensive*). As we said in section 3, we did not attempt to further specify these relations to avoid any commitment to controversial ontologies of property types. Note that we exclude synonymy both because of the inherent problems in this very notion (Cruse, 1986), and because it is impossible to find convincing synonyms for 200 concrete concepts.

In BLESS, we have adopted the simplifying assumption that each relation type has relata belonging to the same part of speech: nouns for *hyper*, *coord* and *mero*, verbs for *event*, and adjectives for *attri*. Therefore, we abstract away from the fact that the same semantic relation can be realized with different parts of speech, e.g., a related event can be expressed by a verb (*transport*) or by a noun (*transportation*).

4.3 Relata

The relata of the non-random relations are English nouns, verbs and adjectives selected and validated by both authors using two types of sources: *semantic sources* (the McRae Norms (McRae et al., 2005), WordNet (Fellbaum, 1998) and ConceptNet (Liu and Singh, 2004)) and *text sources* (Wikipedia and the Web-derived ukWaC corpus, see Section 4.4 below). These resources greatly differ in dimension, origin and content and therefore provide complementary views on relata. Their relative contribution to BLESS also depends on the type of relation and the target concept. For instance, the rich taxonomic structure of WordNet has been the main source of information for many technical hypernyms (e.g. *gymnosperm*, *oscine*), which instead are missing from more commonsense-oriented resources such as the McRae Norms and ConceptNet. Meronyms are rarer in WordNet, and were collected mainly from the latter two resources, with many technical terms (e.g., parts of ships, weapons) harvested from the Wikipedia entries for the target concepts.

Attributes and events were collected from McRae

Norms, ConceptNet and ukWaC. In the McRae Norms, the number of features per concept is fairly limited, but they correspond to highly distinctive, prototypical and cognitively salient properties. ConceptNet instead provides a much wider array of associated events and attributes that are part of our commonsense knowledge about the target concepts (e.g., the events *park*, *steal* and *break*, etc. for *car*). ConceptNet relations such as *Created_by*, *Used_for*, *Capable_of* etc. have been analyzed to identify potential event relata, while the *Has_property* relation has been inspected to look for attributes. The most salient adjectival and verbal collocates of the target nouns in the ukWaC corpus were also used to identify associated attributes and events. For instance, the target concept *elephant* is not attested in the McRae Norms and has few properties in ConceptNet. Thus, many of its related events have been harvested from ukWaC. They include verbs such as *hunt*, *kill*, etc. which are quite salient and frequent with respect to elephants, although they can hardly be defined as prototypical properties of this animal. As a result of the combined use of such different types of sources, the BLESS relata are representative of a wide spectrum of semantic information about the target concepts: they include domain-specific terms side by side to commonsense ones, very distinctive features of a concept (e.g., *hoot* for *owl*) together with attributes and events that are instead shared by a whole class of concepts (e.g., all animals have relata such as *eat*, *feed*, and *live*), prototypical features as well as events and attributes that are statistically salient for the target, etc.

In many cases, the concept properties contained in semantic sources are expressed with phrases, e.g., *lay eggs*, *eat grass*, *live in Africa*, etc. We decided, however, to keep only single-word relata in BLESS, because DSMs are typically populated with single words, and, when they are not, they differ in the kinds of multi-word elements they store. Therefore, phrasal relata have always been reduced to their head: a verb for properties expressed by a verb phrase, and a noun for properties expressed by a noun phrase. For instance, from the property *lay eggs*, we derived the event relatum *lay*.

To extract the random relata, we adopted the following procedure. For each relatum that instantiates a true relation with the concept, we also randomly picked from our combined corpus (cf. Section 4.4) another lemma with the same part of speech, and frequency within 1 absolute logarithmic unit from the frequency of the corresponding true relatum. Since picking a random term does not guarantee that it will not be related to the concept, we filtered the extracted list by crowdsourcing, using the Amazon Mechanical Turk via the CrowdFlower interface (CF).[1] We presented CF workers with the list of about 15K concept+random-term pairs selected with the procedure we just described, plus a manually checked validation set (a "gold set" in CF terminology) comprised of 500 concept+true-relatum pairs and 500 concept+random-term pairs (these elements are used by CF to determine the reliability of workers, and discard the ratings of unreliable ones), plus a further set of 1.5K manually checked concept+true-relatum pairs to make the random-true distribution less skewed. The workers' task was, for each pair, to check a YES radio button if they thought there is a relation between the words, NO otherwise. The words were annotated with their part of speech, and workers were instructed to pay attention to this information when making their choices. Extensive commented examples of both related pairs and unrelated ones were also provided in the instruction page. A minimum of 2 CF workers rated each pair, and, conservatively, we preserved only those items (about 12K) that were unanimously rated as unrelated to their concept by the judges. See Table 1 for summary statistics about the preserved random sets (nouns: RAND.N, adjectives: RAN.J, verbs:RAN.V).

4.4 BLESS statistics

For frequency information, we rely on the combination of the freely available ukWaC and Wackypedia corpora (size: 1.915B and 820M tokens, respectively).[2] The data set contains 200 concepts that have a mean corpus frequency of 53K occurrences (min. 1416 *chisel*, max. 793K *car*). The relata of these concepts (26,554 in total) are distributed as reported in Table 1.

Note that the distributions reflect certain "natural" differences between relations (hypernyms tend to be more frequent words than coordinates, but there are

[1] http://crowdflower.com/

[2] http://wacky.sslmit.unibo.it/

relation	*frequency* *min*	*avg*	*max*	*cardinality* *min*	*avg*	*max*
COORD	0	37K	1.7M	6	17.1	35
HYPER	31	138K	1.9M	2	6.7	15
MERO	0	133K	2M	2	14.7	53
ATTRI	0	501K	3.7M	4	13.6	27
EVENT	0	517K	5.4M	6	19.1	40
RAN.N	0	92K	2.4M	16	32.9	67
RAN.J	1	472K	4.5M	3	10.9	24
RAN.V	1	508K	7.7M	4	16.3	34

Table 1: Distribution (minimum, mean and maximum) of the relata of all BLESS concepts: the *frequency* columns report summary statistics for corpus counts across relata instantiating a relation; the *cardinality* columns report summary statistics for number of relata instantiating a relation across the 200 concepts, only considering relata with corpus frequency ≥ 100.

more coordinates than hypernyms, etc.). Instead of trying to artificially control for these differences, we assess their impact in Section 5 by looking at the behavior of baselines that exploit the frequency and cardinality of relations as proxies to semantic similarity (such factors could also be entered as regressors in a linear model).

5 Evaluation

This section illustrates one possible way to use BLESS to explore and evaluate DSMs. Given the similarity scores provided by a model for a concept with all its relata across all relations, we pick the relatum with the highest score (nearest neighbour) for each relation (see discussion in Section 3 above on why we allow models to pick their favorite from a set of relata instantiating the same relation). In this way, for each of the 200 BLESS concepts, we obtain 8 similarity scores, one per relation. In order to factor out concept-specific effects that might add to the overall score variance (for example, a frequent concept might have a denser neighborhood than a rarer one, and consequently the nearest relatum scores of the former are trivially higher than those of the latter), we transform the 8 similarity scores of each concept onto standardized z scores (mean: 0; s.d: 1) by subtracting from each their mean, and dividing by their standard deviation. After this transformation, we produce a **boxplot** summarizing the distribution of scores per relation across the 200 concepts (i.e., each box of the plot summarizes the distribution of the 200 standardized scores picked for each relation). Our boxplots (see examples in Fig. 1 below) display the median of a distribution as a thick horizontal line within a box extending from the first to the third quartile, with whiskers covering 1.5 of the interquartile range in each direction from the box, and values outside this extended range – extreme outliers – plotted as circles (these are the default boxplotting option of the R statistical package).[3] While the boxplots are extremely informative about the relation types that are best captured by models, we expect some degree of overlap among the distributions of different relations, and in such cases we might want to ask whether a certain model assigns significantly higher scores to one relation rather than another (for example, to *coordinates* rather than *random nouns*). It is difficult to decide *a priori* which pairwise statistical comparisons will be interesting. We thus take a conservative approach in which we perform *all* pairwise comparisons using the **Tukey Honestly Significant Difference** test, that is similar to the standard t test, but accounts for the greater likelihood of Type I errors when multiple comparisons are performed (Abdi and Williams, 2010). We only report the Tukey test results for those comparisons that are of interest in the analysis of the boxplots, using the standard $\alpha = 0.05$ significance threshold.

5.1 Models

Occurrence and co-occurrence statistics for all models are extracted from the combined ukWaC and Wackypedia corpora (see Section 4.4 above). We exploit the automated morphosyntactic annotation of the corpora by building our DSMs out of lemmas (instead of inflected words), and relying on part of speech information.

Baselines. The **RelatumFrequency** baseline uses the frequency of occurrence of a relatum as a surrogate of its cosine with the concept. With this approach, we want to verify that the unequal frequency distribution across relations (see Table 1 above) is not trivially sufficient to differentiate relation classes in a semantically interesting way. For our second baseline, we assign a random number as cosine sur-

[3] `http://www.r-project.org/`

rogate to each relatum (to smooth these random values, we generate them by first sampling, for each relatum, 10K random variates from a uniform distribution, and then averaging them). If the set of relata instantiating a certain relation is larger, it is more likely that it will contain the highest random value. Thus, this **RelationCardinality** baseline will favor relations that tend to have large relata set across concepts, controlling for effects due to different cardinalities across semantic relations (again, see Table 1 above).

DSMs. We choose a few ways to construct DSMs for illustrative purposes only. All the models contain vector representations for the same words, namely, approximately, the top 20K most frequent nouns, 5K most frequent adjectives and 5K most frequent verbs in the combined corpora. All the models use Local Mutual Information (Evert, 2005; Baroni and Lenci, 2010) to weight raw co-occurrence counts (this association measure is obtained by multiplying the raw count by Pointwise Mutual Information, and it is a close approximation to the Log-Likelihood Ratio). Three DSMs are based on counting co-occurrences with collocates within a window of fixed width, in the tradition of HAL (Lund and Burgess, 1996) and many later models. The **ContentWindow2** model records sentence-internal co-occurrence with the nearest 2 content words to the left and right of each target concept (the same 30K target nouns, verbs and adjectives are also employed as context content words). **ContentWindow20** is like ContentWindow2, but considers a larger window of 20 words to the left and right of the target. **AllWindow2** adopts the same window of ContentWindow2, but considers all co-occurrences, not only those with content words. The **Document** model, finally, is based on a (Local-Mutual-Information transformed) word-by-document matrix, recording the distribution of the 30K target words across the documents in the concatenated corpus. This DSM is thus akin to traditional Latent Semantic Analysis (Landauer and Dumais, 1997), without dimensionality reduction. The content-window-based models have, by construction, about 30K dimensions. The other models are much larger, and for practical reasons we only keep 1 million dimensions (those that account, cumulatively, for the largest proportion of the overall Local Mutual Information mass).

5.2 Results

The concept-by-concept z-normalized distributions of cosines of relata instantiating each of our relations are presented, for each of the example models, in Fig. 1. The RelatumFrequency baseline shows a preference for adjectives and verbs in general, independently of whether they are meaningful (attributes, events) or not (random adjectives and verbs), reflecting the higher frequencies of adjectives and verbs in BLESS (Table 1). The RelationCardinality baseline produces even less interesting results, with a strong preference for random nouns, followed by coordinates, events and random verbs (as predicted by the distribution in Table 1). We can conclude that the semantically meaningful patterns produced by the other models cannot be explained by trivial differences in relatum frequency or relation cardinality in the BLESS data set.

Moving then to the real DSMs, ContentWindow2 essentially partitions the relations into 3 groups: coordinates are the closest relata, which makes sense since they are, taxonomically, the most similar entities to target concepts. They are followed by (but significantly closer to the concept than) events, hypernyms and meronyms (events and hypernyms significantly above meronyms). Next come the attributes (significantly lower cosines than all relation types above). All the meaningful relata are significantly closer to the concepts than the random relata. Similar patterns can be observed in the ContentWindow20 distribution, however in this case the events, while still significantly below the coordinates, are significantly above the (statistically indistinguishable) hypernym, meronym and attribute set. Again, all meaningful relata are above the random ones. Both content-window-based models provide reasonable results, with ContentWindow2 being probably closer to our "ontological" intuitions. The high ranking of events is probably explained by the fact that a nominal concept will often appear as subject or object of verbs expressing associated events (*dog barks*, *fishing tuna*), and thus the corresponding verbs will share even relatively narrow context windows with the concept noun. The AllWindow2 distribution probably reflects the fact that many contexts picked by this DSM are function

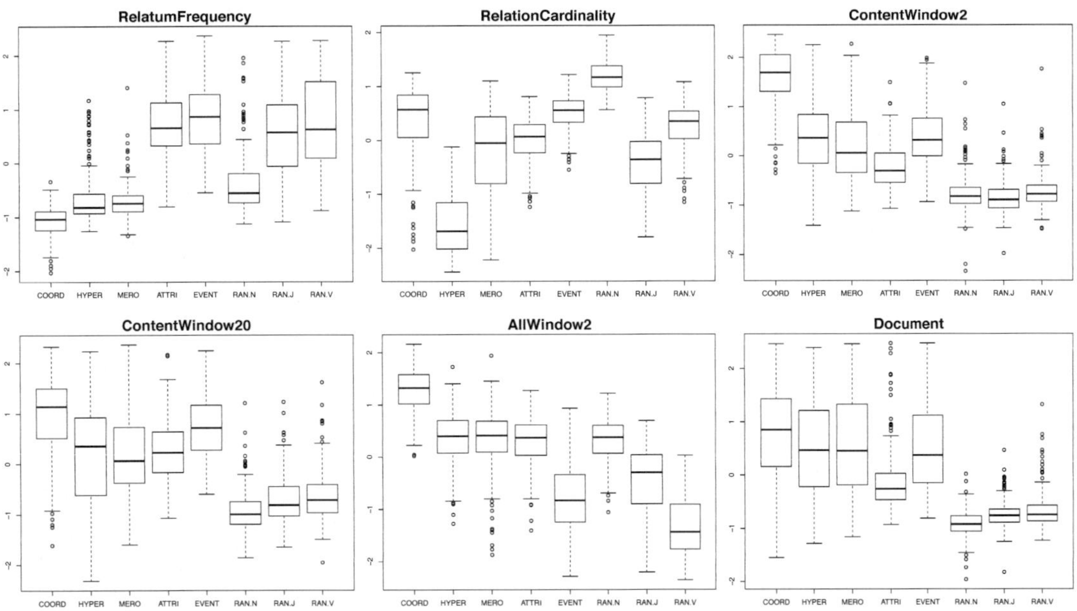

Figure 1: Distribution of relata cosines across concepts (values on ordinate are cosines after concept-by-concept z-normalization).

words, and thus they capture syntactic, rather than semantic distributional properties. As a result, random nouns are as high (statistically indistinguishable from) hypernyms and meronyms. Interestingly, attributes also belong to this subset of relations – probably due to the effect of determiners, quantifiers and other DP-initial function words, that will often occur both before nouns and before adjectives. Indeed, even random adjectives, although significantly below the other relations we discussed, are significantly above both random and meaningful verbs (i.e., events). For the Document model, all meaningful relations are significantly above the random ones. However, coordinates, while still the nearest neighbours (significantly closer than all other relations) are much less distinct than in the window-based models. Note that we cannot say *a priori* that ContentWindow2 is better than Document because it favors coordinates. However, while they are both able to sort out true and random relata, the latter shows a weaker ability to discriminate among different types of semantic relations (co-occurring within a document is indeed a much looser cue to similarity than specifically co-occurring within a narrow window). Traditional DSM tests, based on a single quality measure, would not have given us this broad view of how models are behaving.

6 Conclusion

We introduced BLESS, the first data set specifically designed for the intrinsic evaluation of DSMs. The data set contains tuples instantiating different, explicitly typed semantic relations, plus a number of controlled random tuples. Thus, BLESS can be used to evaluate both the ability of DSMs to discriminate truly related word pairs, and to perform in-depth analyses of the types of semantic relata that different models tend to favor among the nearest neighbors of a target concept. Even a simple comparison of the performance of a few DSMs on BLESS - like the one we have shown here - is able to highlight interesting differences in the semantic spaces produced by the various models. The success of BLESS will obviously depend on whether it will become a reference model for the evaluation of DSMs, something that can not be foreseen *a priori*. Whatever its destiny, we believe that the BLESS approach can boost and innovate evaluation in distributional semantics, as a key condition to get at a deeper understanding of its potentialities as a viable model for meaning.

References

Herv Abdi and Lynne Williams. 2010. Newman-Keuls and Tukey test. In N.J. Salkind, D.M. Dougherty, and B. Frey, editors, *Encyclopedia of Research Design*. Sage, Thousand Oaks, CA.

Eneko Agirre, Enrique Alfonseca, Keith Hall, Jana Kravalova, Marius Paşca, and Aitor Soroa. 2009. A study on similarity and relatedness using distributional and WordNet-based approaches. In *Proceedings of HLT-NAACL*, pages 19–27, Boulder, CO.

Abdulrahman Almuhareb. 2006. *Attributes in Lexical Acquisition*. Phd thesis, University of Essex.

Marco Baroni and Alessandro Lenci. 2010. Distributional Memory: A general framework for corpus-based semantics. *Computational Linguistics*, 36(4):673–721.

Marco Baroni, Stefan Evert, and Alessandro Lenci, editors. 2008. *Bridging the Gap between Semantic Theory and Computational Simulations: Proceedings of the ESSLLI Workshop on Distributional Lexical Semantic*. FOLLI, Hamburg.

Marco Baroni, Eduard Barbu, Brian Murphy, and Massimo Poesio. 2010. Strudel: A distributional semantic model based on properties and types. *Cognitive Science*, 34(2):222–254.

Alexander Budanitsky and Graeme Hirst. 2006. Evaluating wordnet-based measures of lexical semantic relatedness. *Computational Linguistics*, 32:13–47.

D. A. Cruse. 1986. *Lexical Semantics*. Cambridge University Press, Cambridge.

Stefan Evert. 2005. *The Statistics of Word Cooccurrences*. Dissertation, Stuttgart University.

Christiane Fellbaum, editor. 1998. *WordNet: An Electronic Lexical Database*. MIT Press, Cambridge, MA.

Lev Finkelstein, Evgeniy Gabrilovich, Yossi Matias, Ehud Rivlin, Zach Solan, Gadi Wolfman, and Eytan Ruppin. 2002. Placing search in context: The concept revisited. *ACM Transactions on Information Systems*, 20(1):116–131.

Thomas Landauer and Susan Dumais. 1997. A solution to Plato's problem: The latent semantic analysis theory of acquisition, induction, and representation of knowledge. *Psychological Review*, 104(2):211–240.

Hugo Liu and Push Singh. 2004. ConceptNet: A practical commonsense reasoning toolkit. *BT Technology Journal*, pages 211–226.

Kevin Lund and Curt Burgess. 1996. Producing high-dimensional semantic spaces from lexical cooccurrence. *Behavior Research Methods*, 28:203–208.

Ken McRae, George Cree, Mark Seidenberg, and Chris McNorgan. 2005. Semantic feature production norms for a large set of living and nonliving things. *Behavior Research Methods*, 37(4):547–559.

George Miller and Walter Charles. 1991. Contextual correlates of semantic similarity. *Language and Cognitive Processes*, 6(1):1–28.

Gregory Murphy. 2002. *The Big Book of Concepts*. MIT Press, Cambridge, MA.

Timothy Rogers and James McClelland. 2004. *Semantic Cognition: A Parallel Distributed Processing Approach*. MIT Press, Cambridge, MA.

Herbert Rubenstein and John Goodenough. 1965. Contextual correlates of synonymy. *Communications of the ACM*, 8(10):627–633.

Karen Sparck Jones and Julia R. Galliers. 1996. *Evaluating Natural Language Processing Systems: An Analysis and Review*. Springer Verlag, Berlin.

Peter Turney and Patrick Pantel. 2010. From frequency to meaning: Vector space models of semantics. *Journal of Artificial Intelligence Research*, 37:141–188.

Peter Turney. 2006. Similarity of semantic relations. *Computational Linguistics*, 32(3):379–416.

Morton E. Winston, Roger Chaffin, and Douglas Herrmann. 1987. A taxonomy of part-whole relations. *Cognitive Science*, 11:417–444.

Comparison of the Baseline Knowledge-, Corpus-, and Web-based Similarity Measures for Semantic Relations Extraction

Alexander Panchenko
Center for Natural Language Processing (CENTAL)
Université catholique de Louvain, Belgium
alexander.panchenko@student.uclouvain.be

Abstract

Unsupervised methods of semantic relations extraction rely on a similarity measure between lexical units. Similarity measures differ both in kinds of information they use and in the ways how this information is transformed into a similarity score. This paper is making a step further in the evaluation of the available similarity measures within the context of semantic relation extraction. We compare 21 baseline measures – 8 knowledge-based, 4 corpus-based, and 9 web-based metrics with the BLESS dataset. Our results show that existing similarity measures provide significantly different results, both in general performances and in relation distributions. We conclude that the results suggest developing a combined similarity measure.

1 Introduction

Semantic relations extraction aims to discover meaningful lexico-semantic relations such as synonyms and hyponyms between a given set of lexically expressed concepts. Automatic relations discovery is a subtask of automatic thesaurus construction (see Grefenstette (1994), and Panchenko (2010)).

A set of semantic relations R between a set of concepts C is a binary relation $R \subseteq C \times T \times C$, where T is a set of semantic relation types. A relation $r \in R$ is a triple $\langle c_i, t, c_j \rangle$ linking two concepts $c_i, c_j \in C$ with a semantic relation of type $t \in T$. We are dealing with six types of semantic relations: hyperonymy, co-hyponymy, meronymy, event (associative), attributes, and random: $T = \{hyper, coord, mero, event, attri, random\}$. We describe analytically and compare experimentally methods, which discover set of semantic relations $\hat{R}$ for a given set of concepts C. A semantic relation extraction algorithm aims to discover $\hat{R} \sim R$.

One approach for semantic relations extraction is based on the lexico-syntactic patterns which are constructed either manually (Hearst, 1992) or semi-automatically (Snow et al., 2004). The alternative approach, adopted in this paper, is unsupervised (see e.g. Lin (1998a) or Sahlgren (2006)). It relies on a *similarity measure* between lexical units. Various measures are available. We compare 21 baseline measures: 8 knowledge-based, 4 corpus-based, and 9 web-based. We would like to answer on two questions: "What metric is most suitable for the unsupervised relation extraction?", and "Does various metrics capture the same semantic relations?". The second question is particularly interesting for developing of a meta-measure combining several metrics. This information may also help us choose a measure well-suited for a concrete application.

We extend existing surveys in three ways. First, we ground our comparison on the BLESS dataset[1], which is open, general, and was never used before for comparing all the considered metrics. Secondly, we face corpus-, knowledge-, and web-based, which was never done before. Thirdly, we go further than most of the comparisons and thoroughly compare the metrics with respect to relation types they provide. We report empirical relation distributions for

[1]http://sites.google.com/site/geometricalmodels/sharedevaluation

each measure and check if they are significantly different. Next, we propose a way to find the measures with the most and the least similar relation distributions. Finally, we report information about redundant measures in an original way – in a form of an undirected graph.

2 Methodology

2.1 Similarity-based Semantic Relations Discovery

We use an unsupervised approach to calculate set of semantic relations R between a given set of concepts C (see algorithm 1). The *method* uses one of 21 similarity *measures* described in sections 2.2 to 2.4. First, it calculates the concept×concept similarity matrix $\mathbf{S}$ with a measure sim. Since some similarity measures output scores outside the interval $[0; 1]$ we transform them with the function $normalize$ as following: $\mathbf{S} \leftarrow \frac{(\mathbf{S} - min(\mathbf{S}))}{max(\mathbf{S})}$. If we deal with a dissimilarity measure, we additionally transform its score $\mathbf{S}$ to similarity as following: $\mathbf{S} \leftarrow 1 - normalize(\mathbf{S})$. Finally, the function $threshold$ calculates semantic relations R between concepts C with the k-NN thresholding: $\bigcup_{i=1}^{|C|} \{\langle c_i, t, c_j \rangle : c_j \in \text{top } k\% \text{ concepts} \wedge s_{ij} \geq \gamma\}$. Here k is the percent of the top similar concepts to a concept c_i, and γ is a small value which ensures than nearly-zero pairwise similarities s_{ij} will be ignored. Thus, the method links each concept c_i with $k\%$ of its nearest neighbours.

Algorithm 1: Computing semantic relations

Input: Concepts C, Sim.parameters P, Threshold k, Min.similarity value γ
Output: Unlabeled semantic relations $\hat{R}$

```
1 S ← sim(C, P) ;
2 S ← normalize(S) ;
3 R̂ ← threshold(S, k, γ) ;
4 return R̂ ;
```

Below we list the pairwise similarity measures sim used in our experiments with references to the original papers, where all details can be found.

2.2 Knowledge-based Measures

The knowledge-based metrics use a hierarchical semantic network in order to calculate similarities. Some of the metrics also use counts derived from a corpus. We evaluate eight knowledge-based measures listed below. Let us describe them in the following notations: c_r is the root concept of the network; h is the height of the network; $len(c_i, c_j)$ is the length of the shortest path in the network between concepts; c_{ij} is a lowest common subsumer of concepts c_i and c_j; $P(c)$ is the probability of the concept, estimated from a corpus (see below). Then, the Inverted Edge Count measure (Jurafsky and Martin, 2009, p. 687) is

$$s_{ij} = len(c_i, c_j)^{-1}; \quad (1)$$

Leacock and Chodorow (1998) measure is

$$s_{ij} = -log\frac{len(c_i, c_j)}{2h}; \quad (2)$$

Resnik (1995) measure is

$$s_{ij} = -log(P(c_{ij})); \quad (3)$$

Jiang and Conrath (1997) measure is

$$s_{ij} = (2log(P(c_{ij})) - (log(P(c_i)) + log(P(c_j))))^{-1}; \quad (4)$$

Lin (1998b) measure is

$$s_{ij} = (\frac{2log(P(c_{ij}))}{log(P(c_i) + log(P(c_j))}; \quad (5)$$

Wu and Palmer (1994) measure is

$$s_{ij} = \frac{2len(c_r, c_{ij})}{len(c_i, c_{ij}) + len(c_j, c_{ij}) + 2len(c_r, c_{ij})}. \quad (6)$$

Extended Lesk (Banerjee and Pedersen, 2003) measure is

$$s_{ij} = \sum_{c_i \in C_i} \sum_{c_j \in C_j} sim_g(c_i, c_j), \quad (7)$$

where sim_g is a gloss-based similarity measure, and set C_i includes concept c_i and all concepts which are directly related to it.

Gloss Vectors measure (Patwardhan and Pedersen, 2006) is calculated as a cosine (9) between context vectors $\mathbf{v}_i$ and $\mathbf{v}_j$ of concepts c_i and c_j. A context vector calculated as following:

$$\mathbf{v}_i = \sum_{\forall j: c_j \in G_i} \mathbf{f}_j. \quad (8)$$

Here $\mathbf{f}_j$ is a first-order co-occurrence vector, derived from the corpus of all glosses, and G_i is concatenation of glosses of the concept c_i and all concepts which are directly related to it.

We experiment with measures relying on the WORDNET 3.0 (Miller, 1995) as a semantic network and SEMCOR as a corpus (Miller et al., 1993).

2.3 Corpus-based measures

We use four measures, which rely on the bag-of-word distributional analysis (BDA) (Sahlgren, 2006). They calculate similarity of concepts c_i, c_j as similarity of their feature vectors $\mathbf{f}_i, \mathbf{f}_j$ with the following formulas (Jurafsky and Martin, 2009, p. 699): cosine

$$s_{ij} = \frac{\mathbf{f}_i \cdot \mathbf{f}_j}{\|\mathbf{f}_i\| \, \|\mathbf{f}_j\|}, \quad (9)$$

Jaccard

$$s_{ij} = \frac{\sum_{k=1}^{N} min(f_{ik}, f_{jk})}{\sum_{k=1}^{N} max(f_{ik}, f_{jk})}, \quad (10)$$

Manhattan

$$s_{ij} = \sum_{k=1}^{N} |f_{ik} - f_{jk}|, \quad (11)$$

Euclidian

$$s_{ij} = \sqrt{\sum_{k=1}^{N} (f_{ik} - f_{jk})^2}. \quad (12)$$

The feature vector $\mathbf{f}_i$ is a first-order co-occurrence vector. The context of a concept includes all words from a sentence where it occurred, which pass a stop-word filter (around 900 words) and a stop part-of-speech filter (nouns, adjectives, and verbs are kept). The frequencies f_{ij} are normalized with Poinwise Mutual Information (PMI): $f_{ij} = log(f_{ij}/(count(c_i)count(f_j)))$. In our experiments we use two general English corpora (Baroni et al., 2009): WACYPEDIA (800M tokens), and PUKWAC (2000M tokens). These corpora are POS-tagged with the TreeTagger (Schmid, 1994).

2.4 Web-based measures

The web-based metrics use the Web text search engines in order to calculate the similarities. They rely on the number of times words co-occur in the documents indexed by an information retrieval system. Let us describe these measures in the following notation: h_i is the number of documents (hits) returned by the system by the query "c_i"; h_{ij} is the number of hits returned by the query "c_i AND c_j"; and M is number of documents indexed by the system. We use two web-based measures: Normalized Google Distance (NGD) (Cilibrasi and Vitanyi, 2007):

$$s_{ij} = \frac{max(log(h_i, h_j)) - log(h_{ij})}{log(M) - min(log(h_i), log(h_j))}, \quad (13)$$

and PMI-IR similarity (Turney, 2001) :

$$s_{ij} = log\left(\frac{h_{ij} \sum_i \sum_j h_i h_j}{h_i h_j \sum_i h_{ij}}\right). \quad (14)$$

We experiment with 5 NGD measures based on Yahoo, YahooBoss [2], Google, Google over Wikipedia, and Factiva [3]; and with 4 PMI-IR measures based on YahooBoss, Google, Google over Wikipedia, and Factiva. We perform search among all indexed documents or within the domain `wikipedia.org` (we denote the latter measures with the postfix -W).

2.5 Classification of the measures

It might help to understand the results if we mention that (1) - (6) are measures of *semantic similarity*, while (7) and (8) are measures of *semantic relatedness*. Semantic relatedness is a more general notion than semantic similarity (Budanitsky and Hirst, 2001). A measure of semantic similarity uses only hierarchical and equivalence relations of the semantic network, while a measure of semantic relatedness also use relations of other types. Furthermore, measures (1), (2), (3), are "pure" semantic similarity measures since they use only semantic network, while (3), (4), and (5) combine information from a semantic network and a corpus.

The corpus-based and web-based measures are calculated differently, but they are both clearly *distributional* in nature. In that respect, the web-based measures use the Web as a corpus. Figure 1 contains

[2] `http://developer.yahoo.com/search/boss/`
[3] `http://www.factiva.com/`

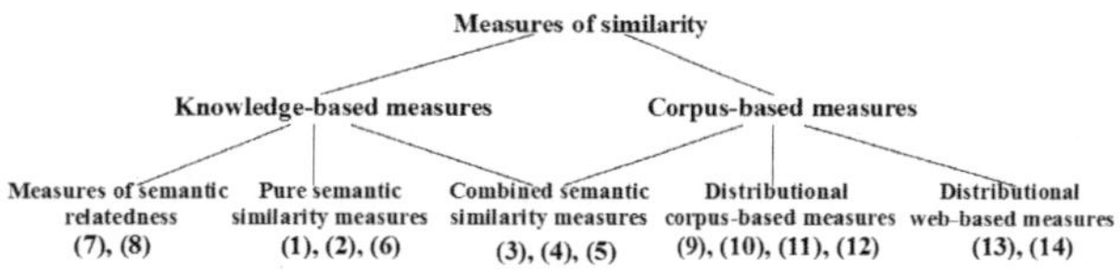

Figure 1: Classification of the measures used in the paper.

a more precise classification of the considered measures, according to their properties. Finally, both (8) and (9)-(12), rely on the vector space model.

2.6 Experimental Setup

We experiment with the knowledge-based measures implemented in the WORDNET::SIMILARITY package (Pedersen et al., 2004). Our own implementation is used in the experiments with the corpus-based measures and the web-based measures relying on the YAHOO BOSS search engine API. We use the MEASURES OF SEMANTIC RELATEDNESS web service [4] to assess the other web measures.

The evaluation was done with the BLESS set of semantic relations. It relates 200 target concepts to some 8625 relatum concepts with 26554 semantic relations (14440 are correct and 12154 are random). Every relation has one of the following six types: hyponymy, co-hyponymy, meronymy, attribute, event, and random. The distribution of relations among those types is given in table 1. Each concept is a single English word.

3 Results

3.1 Comparing General Performance of the Similarity Measures

In our evaluation semantic relations extraction was viewed as a retrieval task. Therefore, for every metric we calculated precision, recall, and F1-measure with respect to the golden standard. Let $\hat{R}$ be set of extracted semantic relations, and R be set of semantic relations in the BLESS. Then

$$Precision = \frac{|R \cap \hat{R}|}{|\hat{R}|}, Recall = \frac{|R \cap \hat{R}|}{|R|}.$$

An extracted relation $\langle c_i, t_?, c_j \rangle \in \hat{R}$ matches a relation from the evaluation dataset $\langle c_i, t, c_j \rangle \in R$ if $t \neq random$. Thus, an extracted relation is correct if it has any type in BLESS, but random.

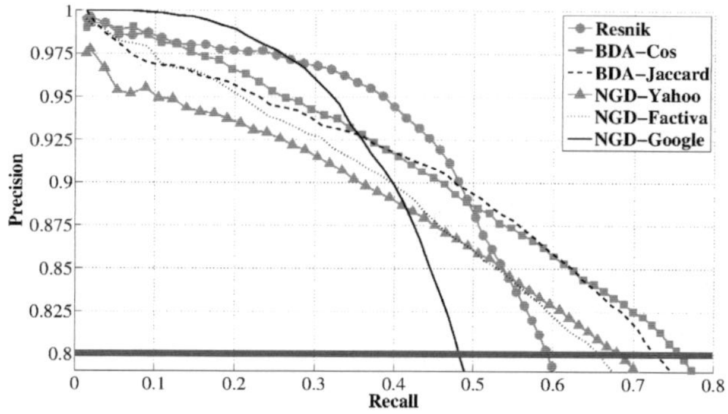

Figure 2: Precision-recall graph of the six similarity measures (kNN threshold value $k = 0 - 52\%$).

General performance of the measures is presented in table 1 (columns 2-4). The Resnik measure (3) is the best among the knowledge-based measures; the NGD (13) measure relying on the Yahoo search engine is the best results among the web-based measures. Finally, the cosine measure (9) (BDA-Cos) is the best among all the measures. The table 2 demonstrate some extracted relations discovered with the BDA-Cos measure.

In table 1 we ranked the measures based on their F-measure when precision is fixed at 80% (see figure 2). We have chosen this precision level, because it is a point when automatically extracted relations start to be useful. It is clear from the precision-recall graph (figure 2) that if another precision level is fixed then ranking of the metrics will change. Analysis of this and similar plots for other measures shows us that: (1) the best knowledge-based metric is Resnik; (2) the BDA-Cos is the best among the corpus-based measures, but BDA-Jaccard is very close to it; (3) the three best web-based measures are NGD-Google (within the precision range 100-90%), NGD-Factiva (within the precision range 90%-87%), and NGD-Yahoo (starting from the precision level 87%). In these settings, choose of the most suitable metric may depend on the application. For instance, if just a few precise relations are needed then NGD-Google is a good choice. On the other hand, if we tolerate a slightly less precision, and if we need many relations then the BDA-Cos is the best choice.

Figure 3 depicts learning curve of the BDA-Cos

[4] http://cwl-projects.cogsci.rpi.edu/msr/

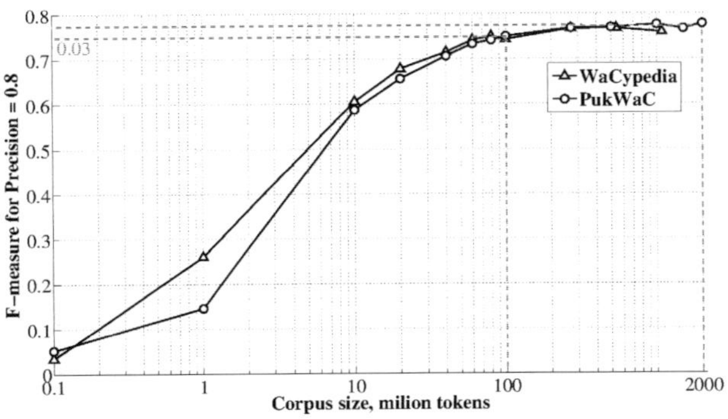

Figure 3: Learning curves of the BDA-Cos on the WaCypedia and PukWaC corpora (0.1M–2000M tokens).

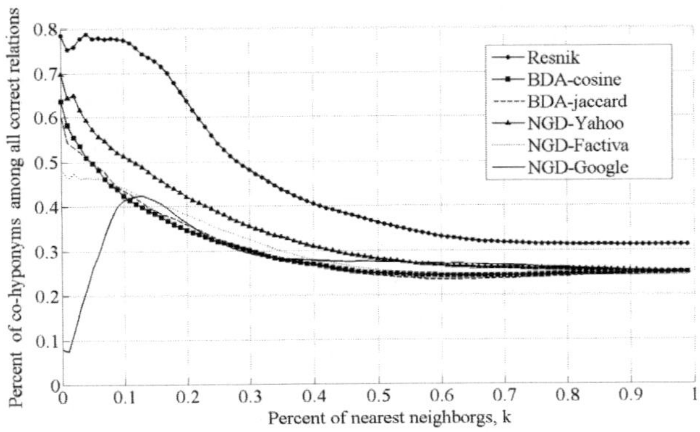

Figure 4: Percent of co-hyponyms among all correctly extracted relations for the six best measures.

measure.Dependence of the F-measure at the precision level of 80% from the corpus size is not linear. F-measure improves up to 44% when we increase corpus size from 1M to 10M tokens; increasing corpus from 10M to 100M tokens gives the improvement of 16%; finally, increasing corpus from 100M to 2000M tokens gives the improvement of only 3%.

3.2 Comparing Relation Distributions of the Similarity Measures

In this section, we are trying to figure out what types of semantic relations the measures find. We compare distributions of semantic relations against the BLESS dataset. Generally, if two measures have equal general performances, one may want to choose a metric which provides more relations of a certain type, depending on the application. This information may be also valuable in order to decide which metrics to combine in a meta-metric.

Distribution of Relation Types. In this section, we estimate empirical relation distribution of the metrics over five relation types: hyponymy, co-hyponymy, meronymy, attribute, and event. To do so we calculate percents of correctly extacted relations of type t for a each measure:

$$Percent = \frac{\hat{R}_t}{|R \cap \hat{R}|}, \text{ where } \bigcup_{t \in T} \hat{R}_t = |R \cap \hat{R}|.$$

Here $|R \cap \hat{R}|$ is a set of all correctly extracted relations, and $\hat{R}_t$ is a set of extracted relations of type t. Figure 4 demonstrates that percent of extracted relations of certain type depends on the value of k (c.f. section 2.1). For instance, if $k = 10\%$ then 77% of extracted relations by Resnik are co-hyponyms, but if $k = 40\%$ then the same measure outputs 40% of co-hyponyms. We report relations distribution at two levels of the threshold k – 10% and 40%.

The empirical distributions are reported in columns 5-9 of the table 1. Each of those columns correspond to one semantic relation type t, and contains two numbers: p_{10} – percent of relations of type t when $k = 10\%$, and p_{40} – percent of relations of type t when $k = 40\%$. We represent those two values in the following format: $p_{10}|p_{40}$. For instance, 77|40 behind the Resnik measure means that when $k = 10\%$ it extracts 77% of co-hypernyms, and when $k = 40\%$ it extracts 40% of co-hypernyms.

If the threshold k is 10% then the biggest fraction of extracted relations are co-hyponyms – from 35% for BDA-Manhattan to 77% for Resnik measure. At this threshold level, the knowledge-based measures mostly return co-hyponyms (60% in average) and hyperonyms (23% in average). The corpus-based metrics mostly return co-hyponyms (38% in average) and event relations (26% in average). The web-based measures return many (48% in average) co-hyponymy relations.

If the threshold k is 40% then relation distribution of all the measures significantly changes. Most of the relations returned by the knowledge-based measures are co-hyponyms (36%) and meronyms (24%). The majority of relations discovered by the corpus-based metrics are co-hyponyms (33%), event relations (26%), and meronyms (20.33%). The web-based measures at this threshold value return many event relations (32%).

	General Performance			Semantic Relations Distribution				
Measure	k	**Recall**	**F1**	**hyper**, %	**coord**, %	**attri**, %	**mero**, %	**event**, %
Resnik	**40%**	**0.59**	**0.68**	**9 | 14**	**77 | 40**	**4 | 8**	**6 | 22**	**4 | 15**
Inv.Edge-Counts	38%	0.56	0.66	22 | 15	61 | 40	4 | 8	7 | 22	6 | 15
Leacock-Chodorow	38%	0.56	0.66	22 | 15	61 | 40	4 | 8	7 | 22	6 | 15
Wu Palmer	37%	0.54	0.65	20 | 15	64 | 42	3 | 8	7 | 22	5 | 13
Lin	36%	0.53	0.64	30 | 16	52 | 31	4 | 7	8 | 29	5 | 16
Gloss Overlap	36%	0.53	0.63	5 | 6	52 | 34	7 | 12	18 | 21	18 | 27
Jiang-Conrath	35%	0.52	0.63	38 | 16	45 | 30	4 | 6	8 | 29	5 | 18
Extended Lesk	30%	0.45	0.57	21 | 14	39 | 30	1 | 9	29 | 28	9 | 19
BDA-Cos	**52%**	**0.76**	**0.78**	**9 | 7**	**42 | 27**	**11 | 20**	**15 | 17**	**23 | 30**
BDA-Jaccard	51%	0.75	0.77	10 | 7	45 | 27	8 | 16	16 | 20	20 | 27
BDA-Manhattan	37%	0.54	0.65	7 | 6	35 | 24	17 | 22	10 | 15	31 | 34
BDA-Euclidian	21%	0.30	0.44	7 | 7	31 | 18	20 | 26	12 | 13	30 | 37
NGD-Yahoo	**46%**	**0.68**	**0.74**	**7 | 6**	**51 | 30**	**9 | 18**	**17 | 20**	**15 | 25**
NGD-Factiva	47%	0.66	0.72	10 | 8	44 | 28	8 | 19	23 | 22	16 | 25
NGD-YahooBOSS	35%	0.51	0.63	13 | 10	54 | 36	4 | 10	14 | 20	15 | 22
NGD-Google	33%	0.48	0.60	1 | 7	41 | 28	45 | 19	2 | 19	11 | 28
NGD-Google-W	29%	0.43	0.56	8 | 9	45 | 31	8 | 14	20 | 21	19 | 25
PMI-YahooBOSS	29%	0.43	0.56	15 | 12	53 | 38	3 | 9	15 | 20	13 | 20
PMI-Factiva	25%	0.28	0.44	8 | 8	42 | 30	10 | 17	21 | 20	18 | 24
PMI-Google	12%	0.18	0.29	8 | 8	55 | 35	7 | 15	17 | 21	12 | 22
PMI-Google-W	9%	0.13	0.23	12 | 11	47 | 38	7 | 11	20 | 20	13 | 19
Random measure				8 | 9	24 | 25	20 | 19	22 | 20	26 | 27
BLESS dataset				9	25	20	19	27

Table 1: Columns 2-4: Recall and F-measure when Precision= 0.8 (correct relations of all types vs random relations). Columns 5-9: percent of extracted relations of a certain type with respect to all correctly extracted relations, when threshold k equal 10% or 40%. The best measure are sorted by F-measure; the best measures are in bold.

ant	**banana**	**fork**	**missile**	**salmon**
cockroach (coord)	mango (coord)	prong (mero)	warhead (mero)	trout (coord)
grasshopper (coord)	pineapple (coord)	spoon (coord)	weapon (hyper)	mackerel (coord)
silverfish (coord)	papaya (coord)	knife (coord)	deploy (event)	herring (coord)
wasp (coord)	pear (coord)	lift (event)	nuclear (attri)	fish (event)
insect (hyper)	ripe (attri)	**fender (random)**	bomb (coord)	tuna (coord)
arthropod (hyper)	peach (coord)	plate (coord)	destroy (event)	oily (attri)
industrious (attri)	coconut (coord)	rake (coord)	rocket (coord)	poach (event)
ladybug (coord)	fruit (hyper)	shovel (coord)	arm (hyper)	catfish (coord)
bee (coord)	apple (coord)	handle (mero)	propellant (mero)	catch (event)
beetle (coord)	apricot (coord)	sharp (attri)	**bolster (random)**	fresh (attri)
locust (coord)	strawberry (coord)	spade (coord)	launch (event)	cook (event)
dragonfly (coord)	ripen (event)	napkin (coord)	deadly (attri)	cod (coord)
hornet (coord)	plum (coord)	cutlery (hyper)	**country (random)**	smoke (event)
creature (hyper)	grapefruit (coord)	head (mero)	strike (event)	seafood (hyper)
crawl (event)	cherry (coord)	scissors (coord)	defuse (event)	eat (event)

Table 2: Examples of the discovered semantic relations with the bag-of-words distributional analysis (BDA-Cos).

Interestingly, for the most of the measures, percent of extracted hyponyms and co-hyponyms decreases as the value of k increase, while the percent of other relations increases. In order to make it clear, we grayed cells of the table 1 when $p_{10} \geq p_{40}$.

Similarity to the BLESS Distribution. In this section, we check if relation distributions (see table 1) are completely biased by the distribution in the evaluation dataset. We compare relation distributions of the metrics with the distribution in the BLESS on the basis of the χ^2 goodness of fit test [5] (Agresti, 2002) with $df = 4$. A random similarity measure is completely biased by the distribution in the evaluation dataset: $\chi^2 = 5.36, p = 0.252$ for $k = 10\%$ and $\chi^2 = 3.17, p = 0.53$ for $k = 40\%$. On the other hand, distributions of all the 21 measures are significantly different from the distribution in the BLESS ($p < 0.001$). The value of chi-square statistic varies from $\chi^2 = 89.94$ (NGD-Factiva, $k = 10\%$) to $\chi^2 = 4000$ (Resnik, $k = 10\%$).

Independence of Relation Distributions. In this section, we check whether relation distributions of the various measures are significantly different. In order to do so, we perform the chi-square independence test on the table 1. Our experiments shown that there is a significant interaction between the type of the metric and the relations distribution: $\chi^2 = 10487, p < 0.001, df = 80$ for all the metrics; $\chi^2 = 2529, df = 28, p < 0.001$ for the knowledge-based metrics; $\chi^2 = 245, df = 12, p < 0.001$ for the corpus-based metrics; and $\chi^2 = 3158, df = 32, p < 0.001$ for the web-based metrics. Thus, there is a clear dependence between the type of measure and the type of relation it extracts.

Most Similar and Dissimilar Measures. In this section, we would like to find the most similar and disimilar measures. This information is particularly useful for the combination of the metrics. In order to find redundant measures, we calculate distance x_{ij} beween measures sim_i and sim_j, based on the χ^2-statistic:

$$x_{ij} = x_{ji} = \sum_{t \in T} \frac{(|\hat{R}_t^i| - |\hat{R}_t^j|)^2}{|\hat{R}_t^j|}, \qquad (15)$$

where $\hat{R}_t^i$ is ensemble of correctly extracted relations of type t with measure sim_i. We calculate these distances for all pairs of measures and then rank the pairs according to the value of x_{ij}. Table 3 present list of the most similar and dissimilar metrics obtained this way. Figure 7 reports in a compact way all the pairwise similarities $(x_{ij})_{21\times21}$ between the 21 metrics. In this graph, an edge links two measures, which have the distance value $x_{ij} < 220$. The graph was drawn with the Fruchterman and Reingold (1991) force-directed layout algorithm. One can see that relation distributions of the web- and corpus-based measures are quite similar. The knowledge-based measures are much different from them, but similar among themselves.

Distribution of Similarity Scores. In this section, we compare distributions of similarity scores across relation types with the following procedure: (1) Pick a closest relatum concept c_j per relation type t for each target concept c_i. (2) Convert similarity scores associated to each target concept to z-scores. (3) Summarize the distribution of similarities across relations by plotting the z-scores grouped by relations in a box plot. (4) Verify the statistical significance of the differences in similarity scores across relations by performing the Tukey's HSD test.

Figure 6 presents the distributions of similarities across various relation types for Resnik, BDA-Cos, and NGD-Yahoo. First, meaningful relation types for these three measures are significantly different ($p < 0.001$) from random relations. The only exception is the Resnnik measure – its similarity scores for the attribute relations are not significantly different ($p = 0.178$) from random relations. Thus, the best three measures provide scores which let us separate incorrect relations from the correct ones if an appropriate threshold k is set. Second, the similarity scores have highest values for the co-hyponymy relations. Third, BDA-Cos, BDA-Jaccard, NGD-Yahoo, NGD-Factiva, and PMI-YahooBoss provide the best scores. They let us clearly ($p < 0.001$) separate meaningful relations from the random ones. From the other hand, the poorest scores were provided by BDA-Manhattan, BDA-Euclidian, NGD-YahooBoss, and NGD-Google, because their scores let us clearly separate only co-hyponyms from the random relations.

Corpus Size. Table 1 presented relation distribution of the BDA-Cos trained on the 2000M token

[5] Here and below, we calculate the χ^2 statistic from the table 1 (columns 5-9), where percents are replaced with frequencies.

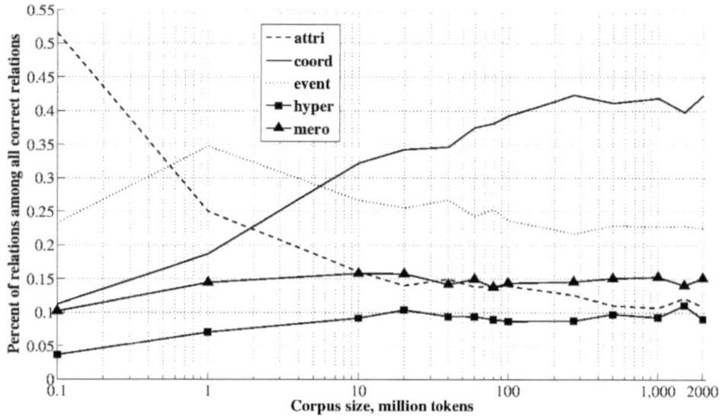

Figure 5: Semantic relations distribution function of corpus size (BDA-Cos measure, PukWaC corpus).

corpus UKWAC. Figure 5 shows the relation distribution function of the corpus size. First, if corpus size increases then percent of attribute relations decreases, while percent of co-hyponyms increases. Second, corpus size does not drastically influence the distribution for big corpora. For instance, if we increase corpus size from 100M to 2000M tokens then the percent of relations change on 3% for attributes, on 3% co-hyponyms, on 1% events, on 0.7% hyperonyms, and on 0.4% meronyms.

4 Related Work

Prior research provide us information about general performances of the measures considered in this paper, but not necessarily on the task of semantic relations extraction. For instance, Mihalcea et al. (2006) compare two corpus-based (PMI-IR and LSA) and six knowledge-based measures on the task of text similarity computation. The authors report that PMI-IR is the best measure; that, similarly to our results, Resnik is the best knowledge-based measure; and that simple average over all 8 measures is even better than PMI-IR. Budanitsky and Hirst (2001) report that Jiang-Conrath is the best knowledge-based measure for the task of spelling correction. Patwardhan and Pedersen (2006) evaluate six knowledge-based measures on the task of word sense disambiguation and report the same result. This contradicts our results, since we found Resnik to be the best knowledge-based measure.

Peirsman et al. (2008) compared general performances and relation distributions of distributional methods using a lexical database. Sahlgren (2006) evaluated syntagmatic and paradigmatic bag-of-word models. Our findings mostly fits well these and other (e.g. Curran (2003) or Bullinaria and Levy (2007)) results on the distributional analysis. Lindsey et al. (2007) compared web-based measures. Authors suggest that a small search domain is better than the whole Internet. Our results partially confirm this observation (NGD-Factiva outperforms NGD-Google), and partially contradicts it (NGD-Yahoo outperforms NGD-Factiva).

Van de Cruys (2010) evaluates syntactic, and bag-of-words distributional methods and suggests that the syntactic models are the best for the extraction of tight synonym-like similarity. Wandmacher (2005) reports that LSA produces 46.4% of associative relations, 15.2% of synonyms, antonyms, hyperonyms, co-hyponyms, and meronyms, 5.6% of syntactic relations, and 32.8% of erroneous relations. We cannot compare these results to ours, since we did not evaluate neither LSA nor syntactic models.

A common alternative to our evaluation methodology is to use the Spearman's rank correlation coefficient (Agresti, 2002) to compare the results with the human judgments, such as those obtained by Rubenstein and Goodenough (1965) or Miller and Charles (1991).

5 Conclusion and Future Work

This paper has compared 21 similarity measures between lexical units on the task of semantic relation extraction. We compared their general performances and figured out that Resnik, BDA-Cos, and NGD-Yahoo provide the best results among knowledge-, corpus-, and web-based measures, correspondingly. We also found that (1) semantic relation distributions of the considered measures are significantly different; (2) all measures extract many co-hyponyms; (3) the best measures provide the scores which let us clearly separate correct relations from the random ones.

The analyzed measures provide complimentary types of semantic information. This suggests developing a combined measure of semantic similarity. A combined measure is not presented here since designing an integration technique is a complex research goal on its own right. We will address this problem in our future research.

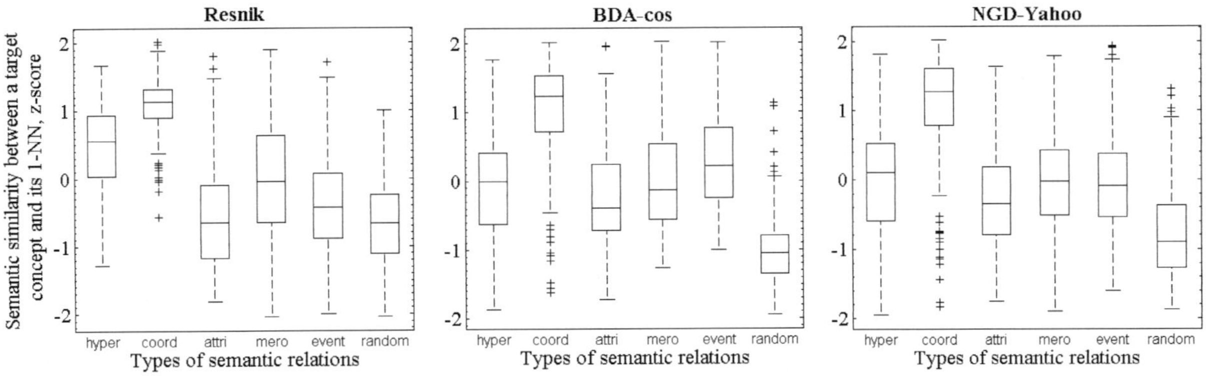

Figure 6: Distribution of similarities accross relation types for Resnik, BDA-Cos, and NGD-Yahoo measures.

Most Similar Measures			Most Disimilar Measures		
sim_i	sim_j	x_{ij}	sim_i	sim_j	x_{ij}
Leacock-Chodorow	Inv.Edge-Counts	0	NGD-Google	Extended Lesk	39935.16
BDA-Jaccard	BDA-Cos	7.17	Jiang-Conrath	NGD-Google	27478.90
NGD-YahooBOSS	PMI-YahooBOSS	19.58	Lin	NGD-Google	17527.22
Wu-Palmer	Inv.Edge-Counts	24.00	NGD-Google	Wu-Palmer	17416.95
Wu-Palmer	Leacock-Chodorow	24.00	NGD-Google	PMI-YahooBOSS	13390.66
BDA-Manhattan	BDA-Euclidian	25.37	Inv.Edge-Counts	NGD-Google	12012.79
PMI-Google-W	NGD-Factiva	27.65	Leacock-Chodorow	NGD-Google	12012.79
PMI-Google	NGD-Yahoo	33.42	NGD-Google	Resnik	11750.41
NGD-Google-W	NGD-Factiva	40.03	NGD-Google	NGD-YahooBOSS	11556.69
NGD-W	PMI-Factiva	42.17	BDA-Euclidian	Extended Lesk	8411.66
Gloss Overlap	NGD-Yahoo	53.64	NGD-Factiva	NGD-Google	8066.75
NGD-Factiva	PMI-Factiva	58.13	BDA-Euclidian	Resnik	6829.71
Lin	Jiang-Conrath	58.42	PMI-Google-W	NGD-Google	6574.62
Gloss Overlap	NGD-Google-W	62.46	BDA-Manhattan	Extended Lesk	6428.47

Table 3: List of the most and least similar measures ($k = 10\%$).

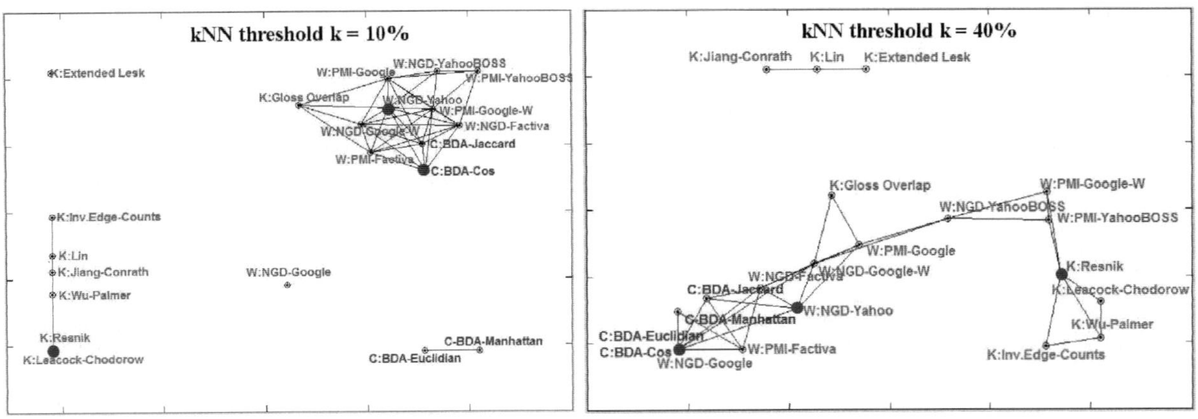

Figure 7: Measures grouped according to similarity of their relation distributions with (15). An edge links measures sim_i and sim_j if $x_{ij} < 220$. The knowledge-, corpus-, and web-based measures are marked in red, blue, and green correspondingly and with the prefixes 'K','C',and 'W'. The best measures are marked with a big circle.

6 Acknowledgments

I would like to thank Thomas François who kindly helped with the evaluation methodology, and my supervisor Dr. Cédrick Fairon. The two anonymous reviewers, Cédrick Fairon, Thomas François, Jean-Leon Bouraoui, and Andew Phillipovich provided comments and remarks, which considerably improved quality of the paper. This research is supported by Wallonie-Bruxelles International.

References

Alan Agresti. *Categorical Data Analysis (Wiley Series in Probability and Statistics)*. Wiley series in probability and statistics. Wiley Interscience, Hoboken, NJ, 2 edition, 2002.

Satanjeev Banerjee and Ted Pedersen. Extended gloss overlaps as a measure of semantic relatedness. In *International Joint Conference on Artificial Intelligence*, volume 18, pages 805–810, 2003.

Marco Baroni, Silvia Bernardini, Adriano Ferraresi, and Eros Zanchetta. The wacky wide web: A collection of very large linguistically processed web-crawled corpora. *Language Resources and Evaluation*, 43(3):209–226, 2009.

Alexander Budanitsky and Graeme Hirst. Semantic distance in WordNet: An experimental, application-oriented evaluation of five measures. In *Workshop on WordNet and Other Lexical Resources*, volume 2, 2001.

John A. Bullinaria and Joseph P. Levy. Extracting semantic representations from word co-occurrence statistics: A computational study. *Behavior Research Methods*, 39(3):510, 2007.

Rudi L. Cilibrasi and Paul M. B. Vitanyi. The Google Similarity Distance. *IEEE Trans. on Knowl. and Data Eng.*, 19(3):370–383, 2007.

James R. Curran. *From distributional to semantic similarity*. PhD thesis, University of Edinburgh, 2003.

Thomas M. J. Fruchterman and Edward M. Reingold. Graph drawing by force-directed placement. *Software: Practice and Experience*, 21(11):1129–1164, 1991.

Gregory Grefenstette. *Explorations in Automatic Thesaurus Discovery (The Springer International Series in Engineering and Computer Science)*. Springer, 1 edition, 1994. ISBN 0792394682.

Marti A. Hearst. Automatic acquisition of hyponyms from large text corpora. In *Proceedings of the 14th conference on Computational linguistics*, pages 539–545, Morristown, NJ, USA, 1992. Association for Computational Linguistics.

Jay J. Jiang and David W. Conrath. Semantic Similarity Based on Corpus Statistics and Lexical Taxonomy. In *International Conference Research on Computational Linguistics (ROCLING X)*, pages 19–33, 1997.

Daniel Jurafsky and James H. Martin. *Speech and Language Processing: An Introduction to Natural Language Processing, Computational Linguistics, and Speech Recognition*. Prentice Hall, 2009.

Claudia Leacock and Martin Chodorow. Combining Local Context and WordNet Similarity for Word Sense Identification. *An Electronic Lexical Database*, pages 265–283, 1998.

Dekang Lin. Automatic retrieval and clustering of similar words. In *Proceedings of the 17th international conference on Computational linguistics-Volume 2*, pages 768–774. Association for Computational Linguistics, 1998a.

Dekang Lin. An Information-Theoretic Definition of Similarity. In *In Proceedings of the 15th International Conference on Machine Learning*, pages 296–304, 1998b.

Robert Lindsey, Vladislav D. Veksler, Alex Grintsvayg, and Wayne D. Gray. Be wary of what your computer reads: the effects of corpus selection on measuring semantic relatedness. In *8th International Conference of Cognitive Modeling, ICCM*, 2007.

Rado Mihalcea, Corley Corley, and Carlo Strapparava. Corpus-based and knowledge-based measures of text semantic similarity. In *Proceedings of the National Conference on Artificial Intelligence*, volume 21, page 775. Menlo Park, CA; Cambridge, MA; London; AAAI Press; MIT Press, 2006.

George A. Miller. Wordnet: a lexical database for english. *Communications of the ACM*, 38(11):39–41, 1995.

George A. Miller and Walter G. Charles. Contextual correlates of semantic similarity. *Language and Cognitive Processes*, 6(1):1–28, 1991.

George A. Miller, Claudia Leacock, Randee Tengi, and Ross T. Bunker. A semantic concordance. In *Proceedings of the workshop on Human Language Technology*, pages 303–308. Association for Computational Linguistics, 1993.

Alexander Panchenko. Can we automatically reproduce semantic relations of an information retrieval thesaurus? In *4th Russian Summer School in Information Retrieval*, pages 13–18. Voronezh State University, 2010.

Siddharth Patwardhan and Ted Pedersen. Using WordNet-based context vectors to estimate the semantic relatedness of concepts. *Making Sense of Sense: Bringing Psycholinguistics and Computational Linguistics Together*, page 1, 2006.

Ted Pedersen, Siddharth Patwardhan, and Jason Michelizzi. WordNet:: Similarity: measuring the relatedness of concepts. In *Demonstration Papers at HLT-NAACL 2004 on XX*, pages 38–41. Association for Computational Linguistics, 2004.

Yves Peirsman, Kris Heylen, and Dirk Speelman. Putting things in order. First and second order context models for the calculation of semantic similarity. *Proceedings of the 9th Journées internationales d'Analyse statistique des Données Textuelles (JADT 2008)*, pages 907–916, 2008.

Philip Resnik. Using Information Content to Evaluate Semantic Similarity in a Taxonomy. In *Proceedings of the 14th International Joint Conference on Artificial Intelligence.*, volume 1, pages 448–453, 1995.

H. Rubenstein and J.B. Goodenough. Contextual correlates of synonymy. *Communications of the ACM*, 8(10):627–633, 1965.

Magnus Sahlgren. *The Word-Space Model: Using distributional analysis to represent syntagmatic and paradigmatic relations between words in high-dimensional vector spaces.* PhD thesis, Stockholm University, 2006.

Helmut Schmid. Probabilistic Part-of-Speech Tagging Using Decision Trees. pages 44–49, 1994.

Rion Snow, Daniel Jurafsky, and Andrew Y. Ng. Learning syntactic patterns for automatic hypernym discovery. *Advances in Neural Information Processing Systems (NIPS)*, 17:1297–1304, 2004.

Peter Turney. Mining the Web for Synonyms: PMI-IR versus LSA on TOEFL. In *Proceedings of the twelfth european conference on machine learning (ecml-2001)*, 2001.

Tim Van de Cruys. *Mining for Meaning: The Extraction of Lexicosemantic Knowledge from Text.* PhD thesis, University of Groningen, 2010.

Tonio Wandmacher. How semantic is Latent Semantic Analysis? *Proceedings of TALN/RECITAL*, 2005.

Zhibiao Wu and Martha Palmer. Verbs semantics and lexical selection. In *Proceedings of the 32nd annual meeting on Association for Computational Linguistics*, pages 133–138. Association for Computational Linguistics, 1994.

Distributional semantics from text and images

Elia Bruni
CIMeC, University of Trento
elia.bruni@unitn.it

Giang Binh Tran
EMLCT, Free University of Bolzano &
CIMeC, University of Trento
Giang.Tran@stud-inf.unibz.it

Marco Baroni
CIMeC, University of Trento
marco.baroni@unitn.it

Abstract

We present a distributional semantic model combining text- and image-based features. We evaluate this multimodal semantic model on simulating similarity judgments, concept clustering and the BLESS benchmark. When integrated with the same core text-based model, image-based features are at least as good as further text-based features, and they capture different qualitative aspects of the tasks, suggesting that the two sources of information are complementary.

1 Introduction

Distributional semantic models use large text corpora to derive estimates of semantic similarities between words. The basis of these procedures lies in the hypothesis that semantically similar words tend to appear in similar contexts (Miller and Charles, 1991; Wittgenstein, 1953). For example, the meaning of *spinach* (primarily) becomes the result of statistical computations based on the association between *spinach* and words like *plant*, *green*, *iron*, *Popeye*, *muscles*. Alongside their applications in NLP areas such as information retrieval or word sense disambiguation (Turney and Pantel, 2010), a strong debate has arisen on whether distributional semantic models are also reflecting human cognitive processes (Griffiths et al., 2007; Baroni et al., 2010). Many cognitive scientists have however observed that these techniques relegate the process of meaning extraction solely to linguistic regularities, forgetting that humans can also rely on non-verbal experience, and comprehension also involves the activation of non-linguistic representations (Barsalou et al., 2008; Glenberg, 1997; Zwaan, 2004). They argue that, without grounding words to bodily actions and perceptions in the environment, we can never get past defining a symbol by simply pointing to covariation of amodal symbolic patterns (Harnad, 1990). Going back to our example, the meaning of *spinach* should come (at least partially) from our experience with spinach, its colors, smell and the occasions in which we tend to encounter it.

We can thus distinguish two different views of how meaning emerges, one stating that it emerges from association between linguistic units reflected by statistical computations on large bodies of text, the other stating that meaning is still the result of an association process, but one that concerns the association between words and perceptual information.

In our work, we try to make these two apparently mutually exclusive accounts communicate, to construct a richer and more human-like notion of meaning. In particular, we concentrate on perceptual information coming from images, and we create a multimodal distributional semantic model extracted from texts and images, putting side by side techniques from NLP and computer vision. In a nutshell, our technique is based on using a collection of labeled pictures to build vectors recording the co-occurrences of words with image-based features, exactly as we would do with textual co-occurrences. We then concatenate the image-based vector with a standard text-based distributional vector, to obtain our multimodal representation. The preliminary results reported in this paper indicate that enriching a text-based model with image-based features is at least not damaging, with respect to enlarging the purely textual component, and it leads to qualitatively different results, indicating that the two sources of information are not redundant.

The rest of the paper is structured as follows. Section 2 reviews relevant work including distributional semantic models, computer vision techniques suitable to our purpose and systems combining text and image information, including the only work we are aware of that attempts something similar to what we try here. We introduce our multimodal distributional semantic model in Section 3, and our experimental setup and procedure in Section 4. Our experiments' results are discussed in Section 5. Section 6 concludes summarizing current achievements and discussing next directions.

2 Related Work

2.1 Text-based distributional semantic models

Traditional corpus-based models of semantic representation base their analysis on textual input alone (Turney and Pantel, 2010). Assuming the distributional hypothesis (Miller and Charles, 1991), they represent semantic similarity between words as a function of the degree of overlap among their linguistic contexts. Similarity is computed in a semantic space represented as a matrix, with words as rows and contextual elements as columns/dimensions. Thanks to the geometrical nature of the representation, words are compared using a distance metric, such as the cosine of the angle between vectors (Landauer and Dumais, 1997).

2.2 Bag of visual words

In NLP, "bag of words" (BoW) is a dictionary-based method in which a document is represented as a "bag" (i.e., order is not considered), which contains words from the dictionary. In computer vision, "bag of visual words" (**BoVW**) is a similar idea for image representation (Sivic and Zisserman, 2003; Csurka et al., 2004; Nister and Stewenius, 2006; Bosch et al., 2007; Yang et al., 2007).

Here, an image is treated as a document, and features from a dictionary of visual elements extracted from the image are considered as the "words" representing the image. The following pipeline is typically adopted in order to group the local interest points into types (**visual words**) within and across images, so that then an image can be represented by the number of occurrences of each visual word type in it, analogously to BoW. From every image of a data set, keypoints are automatically detected and represented as vectors of various descriptors. Keypoint vectors are then projected into a common space and grouped into a number of clusters. Each cluster is treated as a discrete visual word (this technique is generally known as vector quantization). With its keypoints mapped onto visual words, each image can then be represented as a BoVW feature vector according to the count of each visual word. In this way, we move from representing the image by a varying number of high-dimensional keypoint descriptor vectors to a representation in terms of a single sparse vector of fixed dimensionality across all images. What kind of image content a visual word captures exactly depends on a number of factors, including the descriptors used to identify and represent local interest points, the quantization algorithm and the number of target visual words selected. In general, local interest points assigned to the same visual word tend to be patches with similar low-level appearance; but these common types of local patterns need not be correlated with object-level parts present in the images. Figure 1 illustrates the procedure to form bags of visual words. Importantly for our purposes, the BoVW representation, despite its unrelated origin in computer vision, is entirely analogous to the BoW representation, making the integration of text- and image-based features very straightforward.

2.3 Integrating textual and perceptual information

Louwerse (2011), contributing to the debate on symbol grounding in cognitive science, theorizes the *interdependency account*, which suggests a convergence of symbolic theories (such as distributional semantics) and perceptual theories of meaning, but lacks of a concrete way to harvest perceptual information computationally. Andrews et al. (2009) complement text-based models with experiential information, by combining corpus-based statistics with speaker-generated feature norms as a proxy of perceptual experience. However, the latter are an unsatisfactory proxy, since they are still verbally pro-

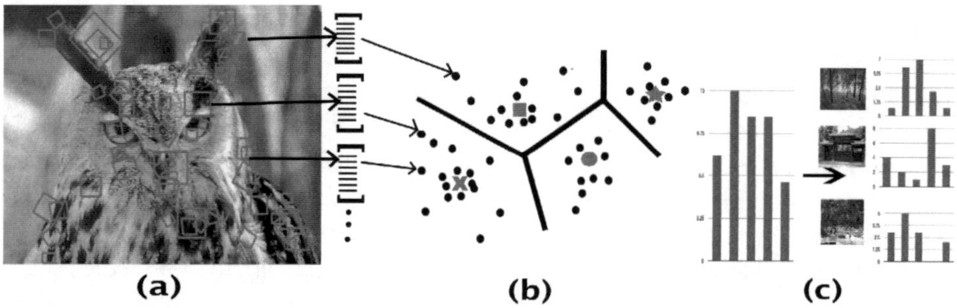

Figure 1: Illustration of *bag of visual words* procedure: (a) detect and represent local interest points as descriptor vectors (b) quantize vectors (c) histogram computation to form BoVW vector for the image

duced descriptions, and they are expensive to collect from subjects via elicitation techniques.

Taking inspiration from methods originally used in text processing, algorithms for image labeling, search and retrieval have been built upon the connection between text and visual features. Such models learn the statistical models which characterize the joint statistical distribution of observed visual features and verbal image tags (Hofmann, 2001; Hare et al., 2008). This line of research is pursuing the reverse of what we are interested in: using text to improve the semantic description of images, whereas we want to exploit images to improve our approximation to word meaning.

Feng and Lapata are the first trying to integrate authentic visual information in a text-based distributional model (Feng and Lapata, 2010). Using a collection of BBC news with pictures as corpus, they train a Topic model where text and visual words are represented in terms of the same shared latent dimensions (topics). In this framework, word meaning is modeled as a probability distribution over a set of latent multimodal topics and the similarity between two words can be estimated by measuring the topics they have in common. A better correlation with semantic intuitions is obtainable when visual modality is taken into account, in comparison to estimating the topic structure from text only.

Although Feng and Lapata's work is very promising and the main inspiration for our own, their method requires the extraction of a single distributional model from the same mixed-media corpus. This has two important drawbacks: First, the textual model must be extracted from the same corpus images are taken from, and the text context extraction methods must be compatible with the overall multimodal approach. Thus, image features cannot be added to a state-of-the-art text-based distributional model – e.g., a model computed on the whole Wikipedia or larger corpora using syntactic dependency information – to assess whether visual information is helping even when purely textual features are already very good. Second, by training a joint model with latent dimensions that mix textual and visual information, it becomes hard to assess, quantitatively and qualitatively, the separate effect of image-based features on the overall performance. In order to overcome these issues, we propose a somewhat simpler approach, in which the text- and image-based models are independently constructed from different sources, and then concatenated.

3 Proposed method

Figure 2 presents a diagram of our overall system. The main idea is to construct text-based and image-based co-occurrence models separately and then combine them. We first describe our procedure to build both text-based and image-based models. However, we stress the latter since it is the more novel part of the procedure. Then, we describe our simple combination technique to integrate both models and create a multimodal distributional semantic space. Our implementation of the proposed method is open-source[1].

[1] `https://github.com/s2m`

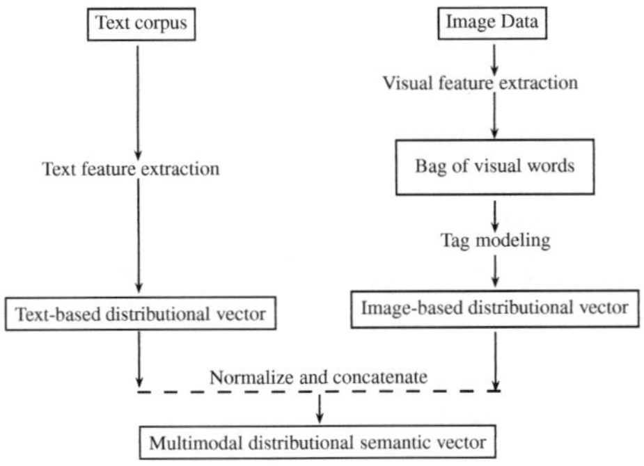

Figure 2: Overview of our system architecture

3.1 Text-based distributional model

Instead of proposing yet another model, we pick one that is publicly available off-the-shelf and has been shown to be at the state of the art on a number of benchmarks. The picked model (**DM**)[2] is encoded in a matrix in which each target word is represented by a row vector of weights representing its association with collocates in a corpus. See Section 4.1 for details about the text-based model.

3.2 Image-based distributional model

We assume image data where each image is associated with word labels (somehow related to the image) that we call **tags**.

The primary approach to form the image-based vector space is to use the BoVW method to represent images. Having represented each image in our data set in terms of the frequency of occurrence of each visual word in it, we construct the **image-based distributional vector** of each tag as follows. Each tag (textual word) is associated to the list of images which are tagged with it; we then sum visual word occurrences across that list of images to obtain the co-occurrence counts associated with each tag. For uniformity with the treatment of textual co-occurrences (see Section 4.1), the raw counts are transformed into Local Mutual Information scores computed between each tag and visual word. Local Mutual Information is an association measure that closely approximates the commonly used Log-Likelihood Ratio while being simpler to compute (Evert, 2005).

In this way, we obtain an image-based distributional semantic model, that is, a matrix where each row corresponds to a tag vector, summarizing the distributional history of the tag in the image collection in terms of its association with the visual words.

[2]`http://clic.cimec.unitn.it/dm`

3.3 Integrating distributional models

We assemble the two distributional vectors to construct the multimodal semantic space. Given a word that is present both in the text-based model and (as a tag) in the image-based model, we separately normalize the two vectors representing the word to length 1 (so that the text and image components will have equal weight), and we concatenate them to obtain the multimodal distributional semantic vector representing the word. The matrix of concatenated text- and image-based vectors is our multimodal distributional semantic model. We leave it to future work to consider more sophisticated combination techniques (preliminary experiments on differential weighting of the text and image components did not lead to promising results).

4 Experimental setup

4.1 The DM text-based model

DM has been shown to be near or at the state of the art in a great variety of semantic tasks, ranging from modeling similarity judgments to concept categorization, predicting selectional preferences, relation classification and more.

The DM model is described in detail by Baroni and Lenci (2010), where it is referred to as TypeDM. In brief, the model is trained on a large corpus of about 2.8 billion tokens that include Web documents, the Wikipedia and the BNC. DM is a structured model, where the collocates are labeled with the link that connect them to the target words. The links are determined by a mixture of dependency parse information and lexico-syntactic patterns, resulting in distributional features (the dimensions of the semantic space) such as *subject_kill*, *with_gun* or *as_sharp_as*. The score of a target word with a feature is not based on the absolute number of times they co-occur in the corpus, but on the variety of different surface realizations of the feature the word co-occurs with. For example, for the word *fat* and the feature *of_animal*, the raw score is 9 because *fat* co-occurs with 9 different forms of the feature (*a fat of the animal, the fat of the animal, fats of animal...*). Refer to Baroni and Lenci (2010) for how the surface realizations of a feature are determined. Raw scores are then transformed into Local Mutual Information values.

The DM semantic space is a matrix with 30K rows (target words) represented in a space of more than 700M dimensions. Since our visual dimension extraction algorithms are maximally producing 32K dimensions (see Section 4.2 below), we make the impact of text features on the combined model directly comparable to the one of visual features by selecting only the top n DM dimensions (with n varying as explained below). The top dimensions are picked based on their cumulative Local Mutual Information mass. We show in the experiments below that trimming DM in this way does not have a negative impact on its performance, so that we are justified in claiming that we are adding visual information to a state-of-the-art text-based semantic space.

4.2 Visual Information Extraction

For our experiments, we use the ESP-Game data set.[3] It contains 50K images, labeled through the famous "game with a purpose" developed by Louis von Ahn (von Ahn and Dabbish, 2004). The tags of images in the data set form a vocabulary of 11K distinct word types. Image labels contain 6.686 tags on average (2.357 s.d.). The ESP-Game corpus is an interesting data set from our point of view since, on the one hand, it is rather large and we know that the tags it contains are related to the images. On the other hand, it is not the product of experts labelling representative images, but of a noisy annotation process of often poor-quality or uninteresting images (e.g., logos) randomly downloaded from the Web. Thus, analogously to the characteristics of a textual corpus, our algorithms must be able to exploit large-scale statistical information, while being robust to noise.

Following what has become an increasingly standard procedure in computer vision, we use the Difference of Gaussian (DoG) detector to automatically detect keypoints from images and consequently map them to visual words (Lowe, 1999; Lowe, 2004). We use the Scale-Invariant Feature Transform (SIFT) to depict the keypoints in terms of a 128-dimensional real-valued descriptor vector. Color version SIFT descriptors are extracted on a regular grid with five pixels spacing, at four multiple scales (10, 15, 20, 25 pixel radii), zeroing the low contrast ones. We chose SIFT for its invariance to image scale, orientation, noise, distortion and partial invariance to illumination changes. To map the descriptors to visual words, we cluster the keypoints in their 128-dimensional space using the K-means clustering algorithm, and encode each keypoint by the index of the cluster (visual word) to which it belongs. We varied the number of visual words between 250 and 2000 in steps of 250. We then computed a one-level 4x4 pyramid of spatial histograms (Grauman and Darrell, 2005), consequently increasing the features dimensions 16 times, for a number that varies between 4K and 32K, in steps of 4K. From the point of view of our distributional semantic model construction, the important point to keep in mind is that standard parameter choices such as the ones we adopted lead to distributional vectors with 4K, 8K, ..., 32K dimensions, where a higher number of features corresponds, roughly, to a more granular analysis of an image. We used the VLFeat implementation for the entire pipeline (Vedaldi and Fulkerson, 2008). See the references in Section 2.2 above for technical details.

4.3 Model integration

We remarked above that the visual word extraction procedure naturally leads to 8 kinds of image-based vectors of dimensionalities from 4K to 32K in steps of 4K. To balance text and image information, we use DM vectors made of *top n* features ranging from 4K to 32K in the same 4K steps. By combining, we obtain 64 combined models (4K text and 4K image dimensions, 4K text and 8K image dimensions, etc.). Since in the experiments on WordSim (Section 5.1 below) we observe best performance with 32K text-based features, we report here only experiments with (at least) 32K dimensions. Similar patterns to the ones we report are observed when adding image-based dimensions to text-based vectors of different dimensionalities.

For a thoroughly fair comparison, if we add n visual features to the text-based model and we notice

[3] `http://www.espgame.org`

an improvement, we must ask whether the same improvement could also be obtained by adding more text-based features. To control for this possibility, we also consider a set of purely text-based models that have the same number of dimensions of the combined models, that is, the top 32K DM features plus 8K, ..., 32K further DM features (the next top features in the cumulative Local Mutual Information score ranking). In the experiments below, we refer to the purely textual model as **text** (always 32K dimensions), to the purely image-based model as **image**, to the combined models as **combined**, and to the control in which further text dimensions are added for comparability with *combined* as **text+**.

4.4 Evaluation benchmarks

We conduct our most extensive evaluation on the **WordSim353** data set (Finkelstein et al., 2002), a widely used benchmark constructed by asking 16 subjects to rate a set of word pairs on a 10-point similarity scale and averaging the ratings (*dollar/buck* receive a high 9.22 average rating, *professor/cucumber* a low 0.31). We cover 260 WordSim (mostly noun/noun) pairs. We evaluate models in terms of the Spearman correlation of the cosines they produce for the WordSim pairs with the average human ratings for the same pairs (here and below, we do not report comparisons with the state of the art in the literature, because we have reduced coverage of the data sets, making the comparison not meaningful).

To verify if the conclusions reached on WordSim extend to different semantic tasks, we use two **concept categorization** benchmarks, where the goal is to cluster a set of (nominal) concepts into broader categories. The Almuhareb-Poesio (**AP**) concept set (Almuhareb, 2006), in the version we cover, contains 230 concepts to be clustered into 21 classes such as *vehicle* (*airplane, car...*), *time* (*aeon, future...*) or *social unit* (*brigade, nation*). The **Battig** set (Baroni et al., 2010), in the version we cover, contains 72 concepts to be clustered into 10 classes. Unlike AP, Battig only contains concrete basic-level concepts belonging to categories such as *bird* (*eagle, owl...*), *kitchenware* (*bowl, spoon...*) or *vegetable* (*broccoli, potato...*). For both sets, following the original proponents and others, we cluster the words based on their pairwise cosines in the semantic space defined by a model using the CLUTO toolkit (Karypis, 2003). We use CLUTO's built-in *repeated bisections with global optimization* method, accepting all of CLUTO's default values. Cluster quality is evaluated by percentage *purity* (Zhao and Karypis, 2003). If n_r^i is the number of items from the *i*-th true (gold standard) class that were assigned to the *r*-th cluster, n is the total number of items and k the number of clusters, then: $\text{Purity} = \frac{1}{n}\sum_{r=1}^{k}\max_i(n_r^i)$. In the best case (perfect clusters), purity is 100% and as cluster quality deteriorates, purity approaches 0.

Finally, we use the Baroni-Lenci Evaluation of Semantic Similarity (**BLESS**) data set made available by the GEMS 2011 organizers.[4] In the version we cover, the data set contains 174 concrete nominal concepts, each paired with a set of words that instantiate the following 6 relations: hypernymy (*spear/weapon*), coordination (*tiger/coyote*), meronymy (*castle/hall*), typical attribute (an adjective: *grapefruit/tart*) and typical event (a verb: *cat/hiss*). Concepts are moreover matched with 3 sets of randomly picked unrelated words (nouns, adjectives and verbs). For each true and random relation, the data set contains at least one word per concept, typically more. Following the GEMS guidelines, we apply a model to BLESS as follows. Given the similarity scores provided by the model for a concept with all associated words within a relation, we pick the term with the highest score. We then z-standardize the 8 scores we obtain for each concept (one per relation), and we produce a boxplot summarizing the distribution of z scores per relation across the concepts (i.e., each box of the plot summarizes the distribution of the 174 scores picked for each relation, standardized as we just described). Boxplots are produced accepting the default boxplotting option of the R statistical package[5] (boxes extend from first to third quartile, median is horizontal line inside the box).

[4] http://sites.google.com/site/geometricalmodels/shared-evaluation

[5] http://www.r-project.org/

5 Results

5.1 WordSim

The WordSim results for our models across dimensionalities as well as for the full *DM* are summarized in Figure 3.

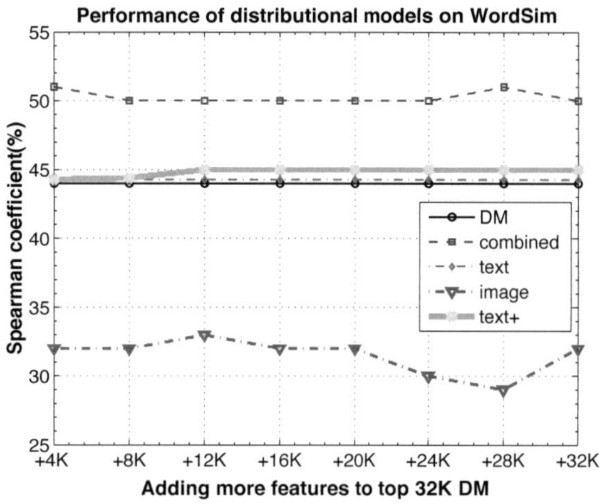

Figure 3: Performance of distributional models on WordSim

The purely image-based model is having the worst performance in all settings, although even the lowest image-based Spearman score (*0.29*) is significantly above chance ($p. < 0.05$), suggesting that the model does capture some semantic information. Contrarily, adding image-based dimensions to a textual model (*combined*) consistently reaches the best performance, also better – for all choices of dimensionality – than adding an equal number of text features (*text+*) or using the full *DM* matrix. Interestingly, the same overall result pattern is observed if we limit evaluation to the WordSim subsets that Agirre et al. (2009) have identified as *semantically similar* (e.g., synonyms or coordinate terms) and *semantically related* (e.g., meronyms or topically related concepts).

Based on the results reported in Figure 3, further analyses will focus on the *combined* model with +20K image-based features, since performance of *combined* does not seem to be greatly affected by the dimensionality parameter, and performance around this value looks quite stable (it is better only at the boundary +4K value, and with +28K, where, however, there is a dip for the *image* model). The *text+* performance is not essentially affected by the dimensionality parameter, and we pick the +20K version for maximum comparability with *combined.*

The difference between *combined* and *text+*, although consistent, is not statistically significant according to a two-tailed paired permutation test (Moore and McCabe, 2005) conducted on the results for the +20K versions of the models. Still, very interesting qualitative differences emerge. Table 1 reports those WordSim pairs (among the ones with above-median human-judged similarity) that have the highest and lowest *combined*-to-*text+* cosine ratios, i.e., pairs that are correctly treated as similar by *combined* but not by *text+*, and *vice versa*. Strikingly, the pairs characterizing the image-feature-enriched *combined* are all made of concrete, highly imageable concepts, whereas the *text+* pairs refer to very abstract notions. We thus see here the first evidence of the complementary nature of visual and textual information.

combined	*text+*
tennis/racket	physics/proton
planet/sun	championship/tournament
closet/clothes	profit/loss
king/rook	registration/arrangement
cell/phone	mile/kilometer

Table 1: WordSim pairs with highest (first column) and lowest (second column) *combined*-to-*text+* cosine ratios

5.2 Concept categorization

Table 2 reports percentage purities in the AP and Battig clustering tasks for full *DM* and the representative models discussed above.

model	*AP*	*Battig*
DM	81	96
text	79	83
text+	80	86
image	25	36
combined	78	96

Table 2: Percentage AP and Battig purities of distributional models

Once more, we see that the *image* model alone is not at the level of the text models, although both its AP and Battig purities are significantly above chance ($p < 0.05$ based on simulated distributions for random cluster assignment). Thus, even alone, image-based vectors do capture aspects of meaning. For AP, adding image features does not improve performance, although it does not significantly worsen it either (a two-tailed paired permutation test confirms that the difference between *text+* and *combined* is far from significance). For Battig, adding visual features improves on the purely text-based models based on a comparable number of features (although the difference between *text+* and *combined* is not significant), reaching the same performance obtained with the full *DM* model (that in these categorization tests is slightly above that of the trimmed models). Intriguingly, the Battig test is entirely composed of concrete concepts, so the difference in performance for *combined* might be related to its preference for concrete things we already observed for WordSim.

5.3 BLESS

The BLESS distributions of text-based models (including *combined*) are very similar, so we use here the full *DM* model as representative of the text-based set – its histogram is compared to the one of the purely *image*-based model in Figure 4.

We see that purely text-based *DM* cosines capture a reasonable scale of taxonomic similarity among nominal neighbours (coordinates then hypernyms then meronyms then random nouns), whereas verbs and adjectives are uniformly very distant, whether they are related or not. This is not surprising because the *DM* links mostly reflect syntactic patterns, that will be disjoint across parts of speech (e.g., a feature like *subject_kill* will only apply to nouns, save for parsing errors). Looking at the *image*-only model, we first observe that it can capture differences between related attributes/events and random adjectives/verbs (according to a Tukey HSD test for all pairwise comparisons, these differences are highly significant, whereas *DM* only significantly distinguishes attributes from random verbs). In this respect, *image* is arguably the "best" model on BLESS. However, perhaps more interestingly, the *image* model also shows a bias for nouns, capturing the same taxonomic hierarchy found for *DM*. This suggests that image analysis is providing a decomposition of concepts into attributes shared by similar entities, that capture ontological similarity beyond mere syntagmatic co-occurrence in an image description.

To support this latter claim, we counted the average number of times that the related terms picked by the *image* model directly co-occur with the target concepts in an ESP-Game label. It turns out that this count is higher for both attributes (10.6) and hypernyms (7.5) than for coordinates (6.5). So, the higher similarity of coordinates in the image model demonstrates that its features do generalize across images, allowing us to capture "attributional" or "paradigmatic" similarity in visual space. More in general, we find that, among all the related terms picked by the *image* model that have an above-average cosine with the target concept, almost half (41%) *never* co-occur with the concept in the image set, again supporting the claim that, by our featural analysis, we are capturing visual properties of similar concepts beyond their co-occurrence as descriptions of the same image.

A final interesting point pertains to the specific instances of each (non-random) relation picked by the textual and visual models: of 870 related term pairs in total, almost half (418) differ between *DM* and *image*, suggesting that the boxplots in Figure 4 hide larger differences in what the models are doing. The randomly picked examples of mismatches in top attributes from Table 3 clearly illustrate the qualitative difference between the models, and, once more, the tendency of *image*-based representations to favour (not surprisingly!) highly visual properties such as colours and shapes, vs. the well-known tendency of text-based models to extract systemic or functional characteristics such as *powerful* or *elegant* (Baroni et al., 2010). By combining the two sources of information, we should be able to develop distributional models that come with more well-rounded characterizations of the concepts they describe.

6 Conclusion

We proposed a simple method to augment a state-of-the-art text-based distributional semantic model with information extracted from image analysis. The method is based on the standard bag-of-visual-words representation of images in computer vision. The image-based distributional profile of a word is

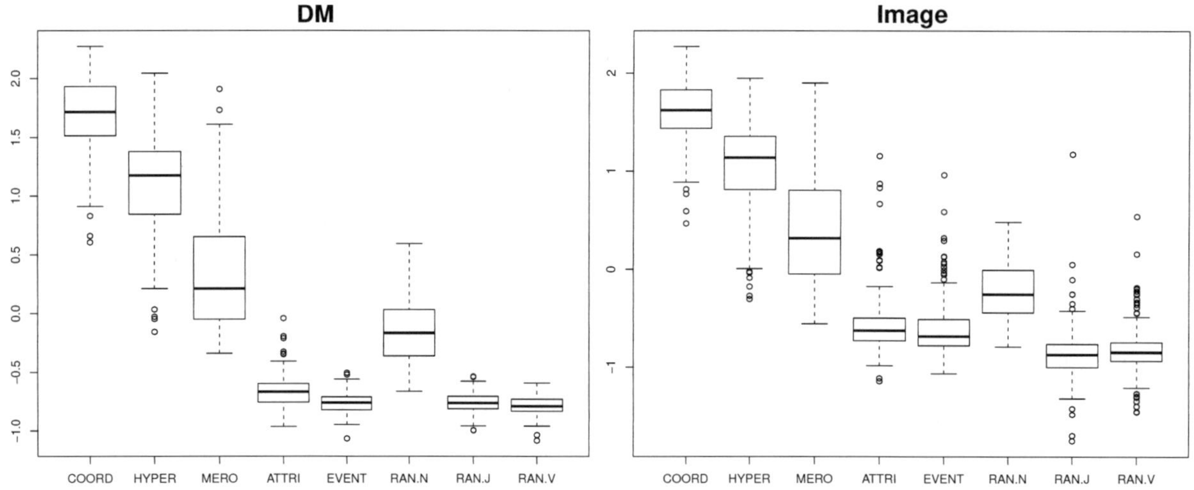

Figure 4: Distribution of z-normalized cosines of words instantiating various relations across BLESS concepts.

concept	*DM*	*image*	*concept*	*DM*	*image*
ant	small	black	potato	edible	red
axe	powerful	old	rifle	short	black
cathedral	ancient	dark	scooter	cheap	white
cottage	little	old	shirt	fancy	black
dresser	new	square	sparrow	wild	brown
fighter	fast	old	squirrel	fluffy	brown
fork	dangerous	shiny	sweater	elegant	old
goose	white	old	truck	new	heavy
jet	fast	old	villa	new	cosy
pistol	dangerous	black	whale	large	gray

Table 3: Randomly selected cases where nearest attributes picked by DM and *image* differ.

encoded in a vector of co-occurrences with "visual words", that we concatenate with a text-based co-occurrence vector. A cautious interpretation of our results is that adding image-based features is at least not damaging, when compared to adding further text-based features, and possibly beneficial. Importantly, in all experiments we find that image-based features lead to interesting qualitative differences in performance: Models including image-based information are more oriented towards capturing similarities between concrete concepts, and focus on their more imageable properties, whereas the text-based features are more geared towards abstract concepts and properties. Coming back to the discussion of symbol grounding at the beginning of the paper, we consider this (very!) preliminary evidence for an integrated view of semantics where the more concrete aspects of meaning derive from perceptual experience, whereas verbal associations mostly account for abstraction.

In future work, we plan first of all to improve performance, by focusing on visual word extraction and on how the text- and image-based vectors are combined (possibly using supervision to optimize both feature extraction and integration with respect to semantic tasks). However, the most exciting direction we intend to follow next will concern evaluation, and in particular devising new benchmarks that address the special properties of image-enhanced models directly. For example, Baroni and Lenci (2008) observe that text-based distributional models are seriously lacking when it comes to characterize physical properties of concepts such as their colors or parts. These are exactly the aspects of conceptual knowledge where image-based information should help most, and we will devise new test sets that will focus specifically on verifying this hypothesis.

References

Eneko Agirre, Enrique Alfonseca, Keith Hall, Jana Kravalova, Marius Paşca, and Aitor Soroa. 2009. A study on similarity and relatedness using distributional and WordNet-based approaches. In *Proceedings of HLT-NAACL*, pages 19–27, Boulder, CO.

Abdulrahman Almuhareb. 2006. *Attributes in Lexical Acquisition*. Phd thesis, University of Essex.

Mark Andrews, Gabriella Vigliocco, and David Vinson. 2009. Integrating experiential and distributional data to learn semantic representations. *Psychological Review*, 116(3):463–498.

Marco Baroni and Alessandro Lenci. 2008. Concepts and properties in word spaces. *Italian Journal of Linguistics*, 20(1):55–88.

Marco Baroni and Alessandro Lenci. 2010. Distributional Memory: A general framework for corpus-based semantics. *Computational Linguistics*, 36(4):673–721.

Marco Baroni, Eduard Barbu, Brian Murphy, and Massimo Poesio. 2010. Strudel: A distributional semantic model based on properties and types. *Cognitive Science*, 34(2):222–254.

Lawrence Barsalou, Ava Santos, Kyle Simmons, and Christine Wilson, 2008. *Language and Simulation in Conceptual Processing*, chapter 13, pages 245–283. Oxford University Press, USA, 1 edition.

Anna Bosch, Andrew Zisserman, and Xavier Munoz. 2007. Image Classification using Random Forests and Ferns. In *Computer Vision, 2007. ICCV 2007. IEEE 11th International Conference on*, pages 1–8.

Gabriella Csurka, Christopher Dance, Lixin Fan, Jutta Willamowski, and Cédric Bray. 2004. Visual categorization with bags of keypoints. In *In Workshop on Statistical Learning in Computer Vision, ECCV*, pages 1–22.

Stefan Evert. 2005. *The Statistics of Word Cooccurrences*. Dissertation, Stuttgart University.

Yansong Feng and Mirella Lapata. 2010. Visual information in semantic representation. In *Human Language Technologies: The 2010 Annual Conference of the North American Chapter of the Association for Computational Linguistics*, pages 91–99, Los Angeles, California. Association for Computational Linguistics.

Lev Finkelstein, Evgeniy Gabrilovich, Yossi Matias, Ehud Rivlin, Zach Solan, Gadi Wolfman, and Eytan Ruppin. 2002. Placing search in context: The concept revisited. *ACM Transactions on Information Systems*, 20(1):116–131.

Arthur Glenberg. 1997. What memory is for. *Behav Brain Sci*, 20(1), March.

Kristen Grauman and Trevor Darrell. 2005. The pyramid match kernel: Discriminative classification with sets of image features. In *In ICCV*, pages 1458–1465.

Tom Griffiths, Mark Steyvers, and Josh Tenenbaum. 2007. Topics in semantic representation. *Psychological Review*, 114:211–244.

Jonathon Hare, Sina Samangooei, Paul Lewis, and Mark Nixon. 2008. Semantic spaces revisited: investigating the performance of auto-annotation and semantic retrieval using semantic spaces. In *Proceedings of the 2008 international conference on Content-based image and video retrieval*, CIVR '08, pages 359–368, New York, NY, USA. ACM.

Stevan Harnad. 1990. The symbol grounding problem. *Physica D: Nonlinear Phenomena*, 42(1-3):335–346, June.

Thomas Hofmann. 2001. Unsupervised Learning by Probabilistic Latent Semantic Analysis. *Machine Learning*, 42(1-2):177–196, January.

George Karypis. 2003. CLUTO: A clustering toolkit. Technical Report 02-017, University of Minnesota Department of Computer Science.

Thomas Landauer and Susan Dumais. 1997. A solution to Plato's problem: The latent semantic analysis theory of acquisition, induction, and representation of knowledge. *Psychological Review*, 104(2):211–240.

Max Louwerse. 2011. Symbol interdependency in symbolic and embodied cognition. *Topics in Cognitive Science*, 3:273–302.

David Lowe. 1999. Object Recognition from Local Scale-Invariant Features. *Computer Vision, IEEE International Conference on*, 2:1150–1157 vol.2, August.

David Lowe. 2004. Distinctive image features from scale-invariant keypoints. *International Journal of Computer Vision*, 60(2), November.

George Miller and Walter Charles. 1991. Contextual correlates of semantic similarity. *Language and Cognitive Processes*, 6(1):1–28.

David Moore and George McCabe. 2005. *Introduction to the Practice of Statistics*. Freeman, New York, 5 edition.

David Nister and Henrik Stewenius. 2006. Scalable recognition with a vocabulary tree. In *Proceedings of the 2006 IEEE Computer Society Conference on Computer Vision and Pattern Recognition - Volume 2*, CVPR '06, pages 2161–2168.

Josef Sivic and Andrew Zisserman. 2003. Video Google: A text retrieval approach to object matching in videos. In *Proceedings of the International Conference on Computer Vision*, volume 2, pages 1470–1477, October.

Richard Szeliski. 2010. *Computer Vision : Algorithms and Applications*. Springer-Verlag New York Inc.

Peter Turney and Patrick Pantel. 2010. From frequency to meaning: Vector space models of semantics. *Journal of Artificial Intelligence Research*, 37:141–188.

Andrea Vedaldi and Brian Fulkerson. 2008. VLFeat: An open and portable library of computer vision algorithms. `http://www.vlfeat.org/`.

Luis von Ahn and Laura Dabbish. 2004. Labeling images with a computer game. In *Proceedings of the*

SIGCHI conference on Human factors in computing systems, CHI '04, pages 319–326, New York, NY, USA. ACM.

Ludwig Wittgenstein. 1953. *Philosophical Investigations*. Blackwell, Oxford. Translated by G.E.M. Anscombe.

Jun Yang, Yu-Gang Jiang, Alexander G. Hauptmann, and Chong-Wah Ngo. 2007. Evaluating bag-of-visual-words representations in scene classification. In James Ze Wang, Nozha Boujemaa, Alberto Del Bimbo, and Jia Li, editors, *Multimedia Information Retrieval*, pages 197–206. ACM.

Ying Zhao and George Karypis. 2003. Criterion functions for document clustering: Experiments and analysis. Technical Report 01-40, University of Minnesota Department of Computer Science.

Rolf Zwaan. 2004. The immersed experiencer: Toward an embodied theory of language comprehension. *Psychology of Learning and Motivation: Advances in Research and Theory, Vol 44*, 44.

Reranking Bilingually Extracted Paraphrases Using Monolingual Distributional Similarity

Tsz Ping Chan, Chris Callison-Burch and **Benjamin Van Durme**
Center for Language and Speech Processing, and HLTCOE
Johns Hopkins University

Abstract

This paper improves an existing bilingual paraphrase extraction technique using monolingual distributional similarity to rerank candidate paraphrases. Raw monolingual data provides a complementary and orthogonal source of information that lessens the commonly observed errors in bilingual pivot-based methods. Our experiments reveal that monolingual scoring of bilingually extracted paraphrases has a significantly stronger correlation with human judgment for grammaticality than the probabilities assigned by the bilingual pivoting method does. The results also show that monolingual distribution similarity can serve as a threshold for high precision paraphrase selection.

1 Introduction

Paraphrasing is the rewording of a phrase such that meaning is preserved. Data-driven paraphrase acquisition techniques can be categorized by the type of data that they use (Madnani and Dorr, 2010). Monolingual paraphrasing techniques cluster phrases through statistical characteristics such as dependency path similarities or distributional co-occurrence information (Lin and Pantel, 2001; Pasca and Dienes, 2005). Bilingual paraphrasing techniques use parallel corpora to extract potential paraphrases by grouping English phrases that share the same foreign translations (Bannard and Callison-Burch, 2005). Other efforts blur the lines between the two, applying techniques from statistical machine translation to monolingual data or extracting paraphrases from multiple English translations of the same foreign text (Barzilay and McKeown, 2001; Pang et al., 2003; Quirk et al., 2004).

We exploit both methodologies, applying a monolingually-derived similarity metric to the output of a pivot-based bilingual paraphrase model. In this paper we investigate the strengths and weaknesses of scoring paraphrases using monolingual distributional similarity versus the bilingually calculated paraphrase probability. We show that monolingual cosine similarity calculated on large volumes of text ranks bilingually-extracted paraphrases better than the paraphrase probability originally defined by Bannard and Callison-Burch (2005). While our current implementation shows improvement mainly in grammaticality, other contextual features are expected to enhance the meaning preservation of paraphrases. We also show that monolingual scores can provide a reasonable threshold for picking out high precision paraphrases.

2 Related Work

2.1 Paraphrase Extraction from Bitexts

Bannard and Callison-Burch (2005) proposed identifying paraphrases by pivoting through phrases in a bilingual parallel corpora. Figure 1 illustrates their paraphrase extraction process. The *target* phrase, e.g. *thrown into jail*, is found in a German-English parallel corpus. The corresponding foreign phrase (*festgenommen*) is identified using word alignment and phrase extraction techniques from phrase-based statistical machine translation (Koehn et al., 2003). Other occurrences of the foreign phrase in the parallel corpus may align to a distinct English phrase, such as *jailed*. As the original phrase occurs several times and aligns with many different foreign phrases, each of these may align to a variety of other English paraphrases. Thus, *thrown into jail* not only paraphrases as *jailed*, but also as *arrested*, *detained*, *imprisoned*, *incarcerated*, *locked up*, and so on. Bad paraphrases, such as *maltreated*, *thrown*, *cases*, *custody*, *arrest*, and *protection*, may also arise due to poor word alignment quality and other factors.

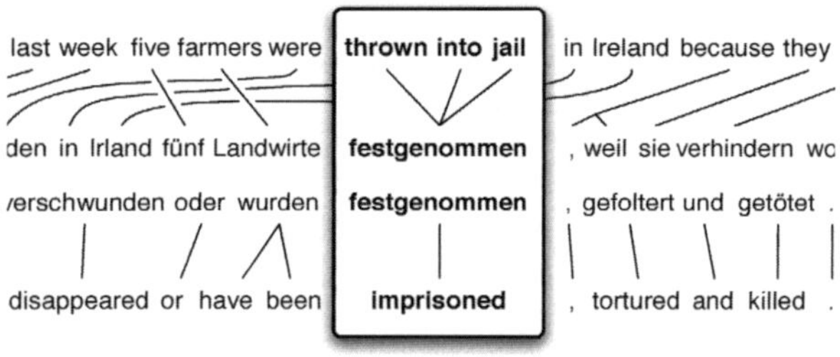

Figure 1: Using a bilingual parallel corpus to extract paraphrases.

Bannard and Callison-Burch (2005) defined a paraphrase probability to rank these paraphrase candidates, as follows:

$$\hat{e_2} = \arg\max_{e_2 \neq e_1} p(e_2|e_1) \quad (1)$$

$$p(e_2|e_1) = \sum_f p(e_2, f|e_1) \quad (2)$$

$$= \sum_f p(e_2|f, e_1)p(f|e_1) \quad (3)$$

$$\approx \sum_f p(e_2|f)p(f|e_1) \quad (4)$$

where $p(e_2|e_1)$ is the paraphrase probability, and $p(e|f)$ and $p(f|e)$ are translation probabilities from a statistical translation model.

Anecdotally, this paraphrase probability sometimes seems unable to discriminate between good and bad paraphrases, so some researchers disregard it and treat the extracted paraphrases as an unsorted set (Snover et al., 2010). Callison-Burch (2008) attempts to improve the ranking by limiting paraphrases to be the same syntactic type.

We attempt to rerank the paraphrases using other information. This is similar to the efforts of Zhao et al. (2008), who made use of multiple resources to derive feature functions and extract paraphrase tables. The paraphrase that maximizes a log-linear combination of various feature functions is then selected as the optimal paraphrase. Feature weights in the model are optimized by minimizing a *phrase substitution error rate*, a measure proposed by the authors, on a development set.

2.2 Monolingual Distributional Similarity

Prior work has explored the acquisition of paraphrases using distributional similarity computed from monolingual resources, such as in the DIRT results of Lin and Pantel (2001). In these models, phrases are judged to be similar based on the cosine distance of their associated context vectors. In some cases, such as by Lin and Pantel, or the seminal work of Church and Hanks (1991), distributional context is defined using frequencies of words appearing in various syntactic relations with other lexical items. For example, the nouns *apple* and *orange* are contextually similar partly because they both often appear as the object of the verb *eat*. While syntactic contexts provide strong evidence of distributional preferences, it is computationally expensive to parse very large corpora, so it is also common to represent context vectors with simpler representations like adjacent words and n-grams (Lapata and Keller, 2005; Bhagat and Ravichandran, 2008; Lin et al., 2010; Van Durme and Lall, 2010). In these models, *apple* and *orange* might be judged similar because both tend to be one word to the right of *some*, and one to the left of *juice*.

Here we calculate distributional similarity using a web-scale n-gram corpus (Brants and Franz, 2006; Lin et al., 2010). Given both the size of the collection, and that the n-grams are sub-sentential (the n-grams are no longer than 5 tokens by design), it was not feasible to parse, which led to the use of n-gram contexts. Here we use adjacent unigrams. For each phrase x we wished to paraphrase, we extracted the context vector of x from the n-gram collection as such: every (n-gram, frequency) pair of the form: (ax, f), or (xb, f), gave rise to the (feature, value) pair: (w_{i-1}=a, f), or (w_{i+1}=b, f), respectively. In order to scale to this size of a collection, we relied on Locality Sensitive Hashing (LSH), as was done previously by Ravichandran et al. (2005) and Bhagat and Ravichandran (2008). To avoid computing feature vectors explicitly, which can be a memory intensive bottleneck, we employed the online LSH variant described by Van Durme and Lall (2010).

This variant, based on the earlier work of Indyk and Motwani (1998) and Charikar (2002), approximates the cosine similarity between two feature vectors based on the Hamming distance in a reduced bitwise representation. In brief, for the feature vectors $\vec{u}$, $\vec{v}$, each of dimension d, then the cosine similarity is defined as: $\frac{\vec{u} \cdot \vec{v}}{|\vec{u}||\vec{v}|}$. If we *project* $\vec{u}$ and $\vec{v}$ through a d by b random matrix populated with draws from

huge amount of		
BiP	**SyntBiP**	**BiP-MonoDS**
large number of, .33	*large number of*, .38	*huge amount of*, 1.0
in large numbers, .11	*great number of*, .09	*large quantity of*, .98
great number of, .08	*huge amount of*, .06	*large number of*, .98
large numbers of, .06	*vast number of*, .06	*great number of*, .97
vast number of, .06		*vast number of*, .94
huge amount of, .06		*in large numbers*, .10
large quantity of, .03		*large numbers of*, .08

Table 1: Paraphrases for *huge amount of* according to the bilingual pivoting (BiP), syntactic-constrainted bilingual pivoting (SyntBiP) translation score and the monolingual similarity score via LSH (MonoDS), ranked by corresponding scores listed next to each paraphrase. Syntactic type of the phrase is [JJ+NN+IN].

$N(0, 1)$, then we convert our feature vectors to *bit signatures* of length b, by setting each bit of the signature conditioned on whether or not the respective projected value is greater than or equal to 0. Given the bit signatures $h(\vec{u})$ and $h(\vec{v})$, we approximate cosine with the formula: $\cos(\frac{D(h(\vec{u}),h(\vec{v}))}{b}\pi)$, where $D()$ is Hamming distance.

3 Ranking Paraphrases

We use several different methods to rank candidate sets of paraphrases that are extracted from bilingual parallel corpora. Our three scoring methods are:

- **MonoDS** – monolingual distributional similarity calculated over the Google n-gram corpus via LSH, as described in Section 2.2.
- **BiP** – bilingual pivoting is calculated as in Equation 4 following Bannard and Callison-Burch (2005). The translation model probabilities are estimated from a French-English parallel corpus.
- **SyntBiP** – syntactically-constrained bilingual pivoting. This refinement to BiP, proposed in Callison-Burch (2008), constrains paraphrases to be the same syntactic type as the original phrase in the pivoting step of the paraphrase table construction.

When we use MonoDS to re-score a candidate set, we indicate which bilingual paraphrase extraction method was used to extract the candidates as prefix, as in **BiP-MonoDS** or **SyntBiP-MonoDS**.

reluctant	
MonoDS$_{hand-selected}$	**BiP**
**willing*, .99	*not*, .56
loath, .98	*unwilling*, .04
**eager*, .98	*reluctance*, .03
somewhat reluctant, .98	*reticent*, .03
unable, .98	*hesitant*, .02
denied access, .98	*reticent about*, .01
disinclined, .98	*reservations*, .01
very unwilling, .97	*reticence*, .01
conducive, .97	*hesitate*, .01
linked, .97	*are reluctant*, .01

Table 2: Ordered reranked paraphrase candidates for the phrase *reluctant* according to monolingual distributional similarity (MonoDS$_{hand-selected}$) and bilingual pivoting paraphrase (BiP) method. Two hand-selected phrases are labeled with asterisks.

3.1 Example Paraphrase Scores

Table 1 shows the paraphrase candidates for the phrase *huge amount of* along with the values for each of our three scoring methods. Although MonoDS does not explicitly impose syntactic restrictions, the syntactic structure of the paraphrase *in large numbers* contributes to the large difference in the left and right context of the paraphrase and of the original phrase. Hence, the paraphrase was assigned a low score of 0.098 as compared to other paraphrase candidates with the correct syntactic type. Note that the SyntBiP produced significantly fewer paraphrase candidates, since its paraphrase candidates must be the same syntactic type as the original phrase. Identity paraphrases are excluded for the rest of the discussion in this paper.

3.2 Susceptibility to Antonyms

Monolingual distributional similarity is widely known to conflate words with opposite meaning and has motivated a large body of prior work on antonym detection (Lin and Zhao, 2003; Lin and Pantel, 2001; Mohammad et al., 2008a; Mohammad et al., 2008b; Marneffe et al., 2008; Voorhees, 2008). In contrast, the antonyms of a phrase are rarely produced during pivoting of the BiP methods because they tend not to share the same foreign translations. Since the reranking framework proposed here begins with paraphrases acquired by the BiP methodology, MonoDS can considerably enhance the quality of ranking while sidestepping the antonym problem that arises from using MonoDS alone.

To support this intuition, an example of a paraphrase list with inserted hand-selected phrases ranked by each reranking methods is shown in Table 2[1]. Hand-selected antonyms of *reluctant* are inserted into the paraphrase candidates extracted by BiP before they are reranked by MonoDS. This is analogous to the case without pre-filtering of paraphrases by BiP and all phrases are treated equally by MonoDS alone. BiP cannot rank these hand-selected paraphrases since, by construction, they do not share any foreign translation and hence their paraphrase scores are not defined. As expected from the drawbacks of monolingual-based statistics, *willing* and *eager* are assigned top scores by MonoDS, although good paraphrases such as *somewhat reluctant* and *disinclined* are also ranked highly. This illustrates how BiP complements the monolingual reranking technique by providing orthogonal information to address the issue of antonyms for MonoDS.

3.3 Implementation Details

For BiP and SyntBiP, the French-English parallel text from the Europarl corpus (Koehn, 2005) was used to train the paraphrase model. The parallel corpus was extracted from proceedings of the European parliament with a total of about 1.3 million sentences and close to 97 million words in the English text. Word alignments were generated with the Berkeley aligner. For SyntBiP, the English side of the parallel corpus was parsed using the Stanford parser (Klein and Manning, 2003). The translation models were trained with Thrax, a grammar extractor for machine translation (Weese et al., 2011). Thrax extracts phrase pairs that are labeled with complex syntactic labels following Zollmann and Venugopal (2006).

For MonoDS, the web-scale n-gram collection of Lin et al. (2010) was used to compute the monolingual distributional similarity features, using 512 bits per signature in the resultant LSH projection. Following Van Durme and Lall (2010), we implicitly represented the projection matrix with a *pool* of size 10,000. In order to expand the coverage of the candidates scored by the monolingual method, the LSH signatures are obtained only for the phrases in the union set of the phrase-level outputs from the original and from the syntactically constrained paraphrase models. Since the n-gram corpus consists of at most 5-gram and each distributional similarity feature requires a single neighboring token, the LSH signatures are generated only for phrases that are 4-gram or less. Phrases that didn't appear in the n-grams with at least one feature were discarded.

4 Human Evaluation

The different paraphrase scoring methods were compared through a manual evaluation conducted on Amazon Mechanical Turk. A set of 100 test phrases were selected and for each test phrase, five distinct sentences were randomly sampled to capture the fact that paraphrases are valid in some contexts but not others (Szpektor et al., 2007). Judges evaluated the paraphrase quality through a substitution test: For each sampled sentence, the test phrase is substituted with automatically-generated paraphrases. The sentences and the phrases are drawn from the English side of the Europarl corpus. Judges indicated the amount of the original **meaning** preserved by the paraphrases and the **grammaticality** of the resulting sentences. They assigned two values to each sentence using the **5-point scales** defined in Callison-Burch (2008).

The 100 test phrases consisted of 25 unigrams, 25 bigrams, 25 trigrams and 25 4-grams. These 25 phrases were randomly sampled from the paraphrase table generated by the bilingual pivoting method, with the following restrictions:

- The phrase must have occurred at least 5 times in the parallel corpus and must have appeared in the web-scale n-grams.
- The size of the union of paraphrase candidates from BiP and SyntBiP must be 10 or more.

4.1 Calculating Correlation

In addition to their average scores on the 5-point scales, the different paraphrase ranking methods were quantitatively evaluated by calculating their correlation with human judgments. Their correlation is calculated using **Kendall's tau coefficient**, a

[1]Generating a paraphrase list by MonoDS alone requires building features for all phrases in the corpus, which is computationally impractical and hence, was not considered here.

Reranking Method	Meaning	Grammar
BiP	0.14	0.04
BiP-MonoDS	0.14	**0.24‡**
SyntBiP	**0.19**	0.08
SyntBip-MonoDS	0.15	0.22‡
SyntBiP$_{matched}$	0.20	0.15
SyntBiP$_{matched}$-MonoDS	0.17	0.16
SyntBiP*	**0.21**	0.09
SyntBiP-MonoDS*	0.16	**0.22†**

Table 3: Kendall's Tau rank correlation coefficients between human judgment of meaning and grammaticality for the different paraphrase scoring methods. Bottom panel: SyntBiP$_{matched}$ is the same as SyntBiP except paraphrases must match with the original phrase in syntactic type. SyntBiP* and MonoDS* are the same as before except they share the same phrase support with SyntBiP$_{matched}$. (‡: MonoDS outperforms the corresponding BiP reranking at p-value $\leq$0.01, and † at $\leq$0.05)

common measure of correlation between two ranked lists. Kendall's tau coefficient ranges between -1 and 1, where 1 indicates a perfect agreement between a pair of ranked lists.

Since tied rankings occur in the human judgments and reranking methods, Kendall's tau b, which ignores pairs with ties, is used in our analysis. An overall Kendall's tau coefficient presented in the results section is calculated by averaging all Kendall's tau coefficients of a particular reranking method over all phrase-sentence combinations.

5 Experimental Results

5.1 Correlation

The Kendall's tau coefficients for the three paraphrase ranking methods are reported Table 3. A total of 100 phrases and 5 sentence per phrase are selected for the experiment, resulting in a maximum support size of 500 for Kendall's tau coefficient calculation. The overall sizes of support are 500, 335, and 304 for BiP, SyntBiP and SyntBiP$_{matched}$, respectively. The positive values of Kendall's tau confirm both monolingual and bilingual approaches for paraphrase reranking are positively correlated with human judgments overall. **For grammaticality, monolingual distributional similarity reranking correlates stronger with human judgments than bilingual pivoting methods.** For example, in the top panel, given a paraphrase table generated through bilingual pivoting, Kendall's tau for monolingual distributional similarity (BiP-MonoDS) achieves 0.24 while that of the bilingual pivoting ranking (BiP) is only 0.04. Similarly, reranking of the paraphrases extracted with syntactically-constrained bilingual pivoting shows a stronger correlation between SyntBiP-MonoDS and grammar judgments (0.22) than the SyntBiP (0.08). *This result further supports the intuition of distributional similarity being suitable for paraphrase reranking in terms of grammaticality.*

In terms of meaning preservation, **the Kendall's tau coefficient for MonoDS is often lower than the bilingual approaches**, suggesting that paraphrase probability from the bilingual approach correlates better with phrasal meaning than the monolingual metric. For instance, SyntBiP reaches a Kendall's tau of 0.19, which is a slightly stronger correlation than that of SyntBiP-MonoDS. Although paraphrase candidates were generated by bilingual pivoting, distributional similarity depends only on contextual similarity and does not guarantee paraphrases that match with the original meaning; whereas Bilingual pivoting methods are derived based on shared foreign translations which associate meaning.

In the bottom panel of Table 3, only paraphrases of the same syntactic type as the source phrase are included in the ranked list for Kendall's tau calculation. The phrases associated with these paraphrases are used for calculating Kendall's tau for the original reranking methods (labeled as SyntBiP* and SyntBiP-MonoDS*). Comparing only the bilingual methods across panels, syntactic matching increases the correlation of bilingual pivoting metrics with human judgments in grammaticality (e.g., 0.15 for SyntBiP$_{matched}$ and 0.08 for SyntBiP) but with only minimal effects on meaning. The maximum values in the bottom panel for both categories are roughly the same as that in the corresponding category in the upper panel ({0.21,0.19} in meaning and {0.22, 0.24} in grammar for lower and upper panels, respectively.) This suggests that syntactic type matching offers similar improvement in grammaticality as MonoDS, although syntactically-constrained approaches have more confined paraphrase coverage.

We performed a one-tailed sign test on the Kendall's Tau values across phrases to examine

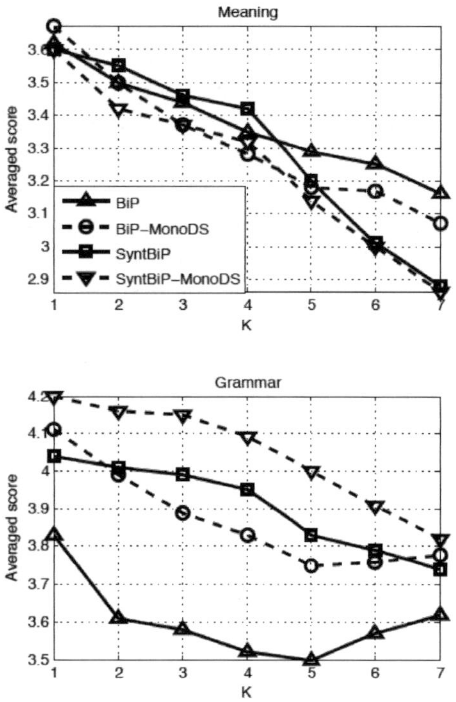

Figure 2: Averaged scores in the top K paraphrase candidates as a function of K for different reranking metrics. All methods performs similarly in meaning preservation, but SyntBiP-MonoDS outperforms other scoring methods in grammaticality, as shown in the bottom graph.

the statistical significance of the performance gain due to MonoDS. For grammaticality, except for the case of syntactic type matching (SyntBiP$_{matched}$), p-values are less than 0.05, confirming the hypothesis that MonoDS outperforms BiP. The p-value for comparing MonoDS and SyntBiP$_{matched}$ exceeds 0.05, agreeing with our conclusion from Table 3 that the two methods perform similarly.

5.2 Thresholding Using MonoDS Scores

One possible use for the paraphrase scores would be as a cutoff threshold where any paraphrases exceeding that value would be selected. Ideally, this would retain only high precision paraphrases.

To verify whether scores from each method correspond to human judgments for paraphrases extracted by BiP, human evaluation scores are averaged for meaning and grammar within each range of paraphrase score for BiP and approximate cosine distance for MonoDS, as shown in Table 4. The BiP paraphrase score bin sizes are linear in log scale.

BiP Paraphrase Score			**MonoDS LSH Score**		
Region	**M**	**G**	**Region**	**M**	**G**
$1.00 \geq x > 0.37$	3.6	3.7	$1 \geq x > 0.95$	4.0	4.4
$0.37 \geq x > 0.14$	3.6	3.7	$0.95 \geq x > 0.9$	3.2	4.0
$0.14 \geq x > 0.05$	3.4	3.6	$0.9 \geq x > 0.85$	3.3	4.0
$0.05 \geq x >$ 1.8e-2	3.4	3.6	$0.85 \geq x > 0.8$	3.3	4.0
1.8e-2 $\geq x >$ 6.7e-3	3.4	3.6	$0.8 \geq x > 0.7$	3.2	3.9
6.7e-3 $\geq x >$ 2.5e-3	3.2	3.7	$0.7 \geq x > 0.6$	3.3	3.8
2.5e-3 $\geq x >$ 9.1e-4	3.0	3.6	$0.6 \geq x > 0.5$	3.1	3.7
9.1e-4 $\geq x >$ 3.4e-4	3.0	3.8	$0.5 \geq x > 0.4$	3.1	3.6
3.4e-4 $\geq x >$ 1.2e-4	2.6	3.6	$0.4 \geq x > 0.3$	3.1	3.5
1.2e-4 $\geq x >$ 4.5e-5	2.7	3.6	$0.3 \geq x > 0.2$	2.9	3.4
$x \leq$ 4.5e-5	2.5	3.7	$0.2 \geq x > 0.1$	3.0	3.3
			$0.1 \geq x > 0$	2.9	3.2

Table 4: Averaged human judgment scores as a function of binned paraphrase scores and binned LSH scores. MonoDS serves as much better thresholding score for extracting high precision paraphrases.

MonoDS LSH	**BiP Paraphrase Threshold**		
Threshold	≥ 0.05	≥ 0.01	$\geq$ 6.7e-3
≥ 0.9	4.2 / 4.4	4.1 / 4.4	4.0 / 4.4
≥ 0.8	4.0 / 4.3	3.9 / 4.3	3.9 / 4.2
≥ 0.7	3.9 / 4.1	3.8 / 4.2	3.8 / 4.1

Table 5: Thresholding using both the MonoDS and BiP scores further improves the average human judgment of Meaning / Grammar.

Observe that for the BiP paraphrase scores on the left panel, no trend on the averaged grammar scores across all score bins is present. While a mild correlation exists between the averaged meaning scores and the paraphrase scores, the top score region ($1 > x \geq 0$) corresponds to merely an averaged value of 3.6 on a 5-point scale. Therefore, thresholding on BiP scores among a set of candidates would not guarantee accurate paraphrases in grammar or meaning.

On the right panel, MonoDS LSH scores on paraphrase candidates produced by BiP are uniformly higher in grammar than meaning across all score bins, similar to the correlation results in Table 3. The averaged grammar scores decreases monotonically and proportionally to the change in LSH values. With regard to meaning scores, the averaged values roughly correspond to the decrease of LSH values, implying distributional similarity correlates weakly with human judgment in the meaning preservation of paraphrase. Note that the drop in averaged scores is the largest from the top bin ($1 \geq x > 0.95$) to the second bin ($0.95 \geq x > 0.9$) is the largest within both meaning and grammar. **This suggests that thresholding on top tiered MonoDS scores can be a good filter for extracting high precision paraphrases.** BiP scores, by comparison, are not as useful for thresholding grammaticality.

Additional performance gain attained by combining the two thresholding are illustrated in Table 5, where averaged meaning and grammar scores are listed for each combination of thresholding. At a threshold of 0.9 for MonoDS LSH score and 0.05 for BiP paraphrase score, the averaged meaning exceeds the highest value reported in Table 4, whereas the grammar scores reaches the value in the top bin in Table 4. General trends of improvement from utilizing the two reranking methods are observed by comparing Tables 4 and 5.

5.3 Top K Analysis

Figure 2 shows the mean human assigned score within the top K candidates averaged across all phrases. Compared across the two categories, meaning scores have lower range of score and a more uniform trend of decreasing values as K grows. In grammaticality, BiP clearly underperforms whereas the SyntBiP-MonoDS maintains the best score among all methods over all values of K. In addition, a slow drop-off up until K = 4 in the curve for SyntBiP-MonoDS implies that the quality of paraphrases remains relatively high going from top 1 to top 4 candidates.

In applications such as question answering or search, the order of answers presented is important because the lower an answer is ranked, the less likely it would be looked at by a user. Based on this intuition, the paraphrase ranking methods are evaluated using the maximum human judgment score among the top K candidates obtained by each method. As shown in Table 6, when only the top candidate is considered, the averaged score corresponding to the monolingual reranking methods are roughly the same as that to the bilingual methods in meaning, but as K grows, the bilingual methods outperforms the monolingual methods. In terms of grammaticality, scores associated with monolingual reranking methods are consistently higher than the bilingual methods but the difference tapers off as K increases. This suggests that when only limited top paraphrase candidates can be evaluated, MonoDS is likely to provide better quality of results.

		Reranking Method			
	K	BiP	BiP-MonoDS	SyntBiP	SyntBiP-MonoDS
M	1	3.62	3.67	3.58	3.58
	3	4.13	4.07	4.13	4.01
	5	4.26	4.19	4.20	4.09
	10	4.39	4.30	4.25	4.23
G	1	3.83	4.11	4.04	4.23
	3	4.22	4.45	4.47	4.54
	5	4.38	4.54	4.55	4.62
	10	4.52	4.62	4.63	4.67

Table 6: Average of the *maximum* human evaluation score from top K candidates for each reranking method. Support sizes for BiP- and SyntBiP-based metrics are 500 and 335, respectively. (M = Meaning, G = Grammar)

6 Detailed Examples

6.1 MonoDS Filters Bad BiP Paraphrases

The examples in the top panel of Table 7 illustrates a few disadvantages of the bilingual paraphrase scores and how monolingual reranking complements the bilingual methods. Translation models based on bilingual corpora are known to suffer from misalignment of the parallel text (Bannard and Callison-Burch, 2005), producing incorrect translations that propagate through in the paraphrase model. This issue is exemplified in the phrase pairs {*considerable changes, caused quite*}, {*always declared, always been*}, and {*significantly affected, known*} listed Table 7. The paraphrases are clearly unrelated to the corresponding phrases as evident from the low rankings from human judges. Nonetheless, they were included as candidates likely due to misalignment and were ranked relatively high by BiP metric. For example, *considerable changes* was aligned to *modifie considérablement* correctly. However, due to a combination of loose translations and difficulty in aligning multiple words that are spread out in a sentence, the French phrase was inaccurately matched with *caused quite* by the aligner, inducing a bad paraphrase. Note that in these cases LSH produces the results that agrees with the human rankings.

Phrase	Paraphrase	Ranking Size$_{pool}$	Meaning	Grammar	BiP	BiP-MonoDS
significantly affected	*known*	20	19	18.5	1	17
considerable changes	*caused quite*	23	23	23	2.5	23
always declared	*always been*	20	20	20	2	13
hauled	*delivered*	23	7	5.5	21.5	5.0
fiscal burden†	*taxes*	18	13.5	18	6	16
fiscal burden†	*taxes*	18	2	8	6	16
legalise	*legalize*	23	1	1	10	1
to deal properly with	*address*	35	4.5	5.5	4	29.5
you have just stated	*you have just suggested*	31	13.5	8.5	4	30

Table 7: Examples of phrase pair rankings by different reranking methods and human judgments in terms of meaning and grammar. Higher rank (smaller numbers) corresponds to more favorable paraphrases by the associated metric. (†: Phrases are listed twice to show the ranking variation when substitutions are evaluated in different sentences.)

6.2 Context Matters

Occasionally, paraphrases are context-dependent, meaning the relevance of the paraphrase depends on the context in a sentence. Bilingual methods can capture limited context through syntactic constraints if the POS tags of the paraphrases and the sentence are available, while the distributional similarity metric, in its current implementation, is purely based on the pattern of co-occurrence with neighboring context n-grams. As a result, LSH scores should be slightly better at gauging the paraphrases defined by context, as suggested by some examples in Table 7. The phrase pair {*hauled, delivered*} differ slightly in how they describe the manner that an object is moved. However, in the context of the following sentence, they roughly correspond to the same idea:

countries which do not comply with community legislation should be ***hauled*** *before the court of justice and i think mrs palacio will do so .*

As a result, out of 23 candidates, human judges ranked *delivered* 7 and 5.5 for meaning and grammar, respectively. The monolingual-based metric also assigns a higher rank to the paraphrase while BiP puts it near the lowest rank.

Another example of context-dependency is the phrase pair {*fiscal burden, taxes*}, which could have some foreign translations in common. The original phrase appears in the following sentence:

... the member states can reduce the ***fiscal burden*** *consisting of taxes and social contributions .*

The paraphrase candidate *taxes* is no longer appropriate with the consideration of the context surrounding the original phrase. As such, *taxes* received rankings of 13.5, 18 and 16 out of 18 for meaning, grammar, and MonoDS, respectively, whereas BiP assigns a 6 to the paraphrase. The same phrase pair but a different sentence, the context induces opposite effects on the paraphrase judgments, where the paraphrase received 2 and 8 in the two categories as shown in Table 7:

the economic data for our eu as regards employment and economic growth are not particularly good , and , in addition , the ***fiscal burden*** *in europe , which is to be borne by the citizen , has reached an all-time high of 46 % .*

Hence, distributional similarity offers additional advantages over BiP only when the paraphrase appears in a context that also defines most of the non-zero dimensions of the LSH signature vector.

The phrase pair {*legalise, legalize*} exemplifies the effect of using different corpora to train 2 paraphrase reranking models as shown in Table 7. Meaning, grammar and MonoDS all received top rank out of all paraphrases, whereas BiP ranks the paraphrase 10 out of 23. Since the BiP method was trained with Europarl data, which is dominated by British English, BiP fails to acknowledge the American spelling of the same word. On the other hand, distributional similarity feature vectors were extracted from the n-gram corpus with different variations of English, which was informative for paraphrase ranking. This property can be exploited for adaptation of specific domain of paraphrases selection.

6.3 Limitations of MonoDS Implementation

While the monolingual distributional similarity shows promise as a paraphrase ranking method, there are a number of additional drawbacks associated with the implementation.

The method is currently limited to phrases with up to 4 contiguous words that are present in the n-gram corpus for LSH feature vector extraction. Since cosine similarity is a function of the angle between 2 vectors irrespective of the vector magnitudes, thresholding on low occurrences of higher n-grams in the corpus construction causes larger n-grams to suffer from feature sparsity and be susceptible to noise. A few examples from the experiment demonstrate such scenario. For a phrase *to deal properly with*, a paraphrase candidate *address* receives rankings of 4.5, 5.5 and 4 out of 35 for meaning, grammar and BiP, respectively, it is ranked 29.5 by BiP-MonoDS. The two phrases are expected to have similar neighboring context in regular English usage, but it might be misrepresented by the LSH feature vector due to the lack of occurrences of the 4-gram in the corpus.

Another example of how sparsity affects LSH feature vectors is the phrase *you have just stated*. An acceptable paraphrase *you have just suggested* was ranked 13.5, 8.5 and 6.5 out of a total of 31 candidates by meaning, grammar and BiP, respectively, but MonoDS only ranks it at 30. The cosine similarity between the phrases are 0.05, which is very low. However, the only tokens that differentiate the 4-gram phrases, i.e. $\{stated, suggested\}$, have a similarity score of 0.91. This suggests that even though the additional words in the phrase don't alter the meaning significantly, the feature vectors are misrepresented due to the sparsity of the 4-gram. This highlights a weakness of the current implementation of distributional similarity, namely that context within a phrase is not considered for larger n-grams.

7 Conclusions and Future Work

We have presented a novel paraphrase ranking metric that assigns a score to paraphrase candidates according to their monolingual distributional similarity to the original phrase. While bilingual pivoting-based paraphrase models provide wide coverage of paraphrase candidates and syntactic constraints on the model confines the structural match, additional contextual similarity information provided by monolingual semantic statistics increases the accuracy of paraphrase ranking within the target language. Through a manual evaluation, it was shown that monolingual distributional scores strongly correlate with human assessment of paraphrase quality in terms of grammaticality, yet have minimal effects on meaning preservation of paraphrases.

While we speculated that MonoDS would improve both meaning and grammar scoring for paraphrases, we found in the results that only grammaticality was improved from the monolingual approach. This is likely due to the choice of how context is represented, which in this case is only single neighboring words. A consideration for future work to enhance paraphrasal meaning preservation would be to explore other contextual representations, such as syntactic dependency parsing (Lin, 1997), mutual information between co-occurences of phrases Church and Hanks (1991), or increasing the number of neighboring words used in n-gram based representations.

In future work we will make use of other complementary bilingual and monolingual knowledge sources by combining other features such as n-gram length, language model scores, etc. One approach would be to perform minimum error rate training similar to Zhao et al. (2008) in which linear weights of a feature function for a set of paraphrases candidate are trained iteratively to minimize the phrasal-substitution-based error rate. Instead of phrasal substitution in Zhao's method, quantitative measure of correlation with human judgment can be used as the objective function to be optimized during training. Other techniques such as SVM-rank (Joachims, 2002) may also be investigated for aggregating results from multiple ranked lists.

8 Acknowledgements

Thanks to Courtney Napoles for advice regarding a pilot version of this work. Thanks to Jonathan Weese, Matt Post and Juri Ganitkevitch for their assistance with Thrax. This research was supported by the EuroMatrixPlus project funded by the European Commission (7th Framework Programme), and by the NSF under grant IIS-0713448. Opinions, interpretations, and conclusions are the authors' alone.

References

Colin Bannard and Chris Callison-Burch. 2005. Paraphrasing with bilingual parallel corpora. In *Proceedings of ACL.*

Regina Barzilay and Kathleen McKeown. 2001. Extracting paraphrases from a parallel corpus. In *Proceedings of ACL.*

Rahul Bhagat and Deepak Ravichandran. 2008. Large scale acquisition of paraphrases for learning surface patterns. In *Proceedings of ACL-HLT.*

Thorsten Brants and Alex Franz. 2006. Web 1T 5-gram version 1.

Chris Callison-Burch. 2008. Syntactic constraints on paraphrases extracted from parallel corpora. In *Proceedings of EMNLP.*

Moses Charikar. 2002. Similarity estimation techniques from rounding algorithms. In *Proceedings of STOC.*

Kenneth Church and Patrick Hanks. 1991. Word association norms, mutual information and lexicography. *Computational Linguistics*, 6(1):22–29.

Piotr Indyk and Rajeev Motwani. 1998. Approximate nearest neighbors: towards removing the curse of dimensionality. In *Proceedings of STOC.*

Thorsten Joachims. 2002. Optimizing search engines using clickthrough data. In *Proceedings of the ACM Conference on Knowledge Discovery and Data Mining.*

Dan Klein and Christopher D. Manning. 2003. Fast exact inference with a factored model for natural language parsing. *Advances in NIPS*, 15:3–10.

Philipp Koehn, Franz Josef Och, and Daniel Marcu. 2003. Statistical phrase-based translation. In *Proceedings of HLT/NAACL.*

Philipp Koehn. 2005. A parallel corpus for statistical machine translation. In *Proceedings of MT-Summit.*

Mirella Lapata and Frank Keller. 2005. Web-based models for natural language processing. *ACM Transactions on Speech and Language Processing*, 2(1).

Dekang Lin and Patrick Pantel. 2001. Discovery of inference rules for question answering. *Natural Language Engineering*, 7:343–360.

Dekang Lin and Shaojun Zhao. 2003. Identifying synonyms among distributionally similar words. In *Proceedings of IJCAI-03*, pages 1492–1493.

Dekang Lin, Kenneth Church, Heng Ji, Satoshi Sekine, David Yarowsky, Shane Bergsma, Kailash Patil, Emily Pitler, Rachel Lathbury, Vikram Rao, Kapil Dalwani, and Sushant Narsale. 2010. New tools for web-scale n-grams. In *Proceedings of LREC.*

Dekang Lin. 1997. Using syntactic dependency as local context to resolve word sense ambiguity. In *Proceedings of ACL.*

Nitin Madnani and Bonnie Dorr. 2010. Generating phrasal and sentential paraphrases: A survey of data-driven methods. *Computational Linguistics*, 36(3).

Marie-Catherine De Marneffe, Anna N. Rafferty, and Christopher D. Manning. 2008. Finding contradictions in text. In *Proceedings of ACL 2008.*

Saif Mohammad, Bonnie Dorr, and Graeme Hirst. 2008a. Computing word-pair antonymy. In *Proceedings of the Conference on Empirical Methods in Natural Language Processing*, pages 982–991. Association for Computational Linguistics.

Saif Mohammad, Bonnie J. Dorr, Melissa Egan, Nitin Madnani, David Zajic, and Jimmy Lin. 2008b. Multiple alternative sentence compressions and word-pair antonymy for automatic text summarization and recognizing textual entailment.

Bo Pang, Kevin Knight, and Daniel Marcu. 2003. Syntax-based alignment of multiple translations: Extracting paraphrases and generating new sentences. In *Proceedings of HLT/NAACL.*

Marius Pasca and Peter Dienes. 2005. Aligning needles in a haystack: Paraphrase acquisition across the web. In *Proceedings of IJCNLP*, pages 119–130.

Chris Quirk, Chris Brockett, and William Dolan. 2004. Monolingual machine translation for paraphrase generation. In *Proceedings of EMNLP*, pages 142–149.

Deepak Ravichandran, Patrick Pantel, and Eduard Hovy. 2005. Randomized Algorithms and NLP: Using Locality Sensitive Hash Functions for High Speed Noun Clustering. In *Proceedings of ACL.*

Matthew Snover, Nitin Madnani, Bonnie Dorr, and Richard Schwartz. 2010. TER-plus: paraphrase, semantic, and alignment enhancements to translation edit rate. *Machine Translation*, 23(2-3):117–127.

Idan Szpektor, Eyal Shnarch, and Ido Dagan. 2007. Instance-based evaluation of entailment rule acquisition. In *Proceedings of ACL.*

Benjamin Van Durme and Ashwin Lall. 2010. Online generation of locality sensitive hash signatures. In *Proceedings of ACL, Short Papers.*

Ellen M. Voorhees. 2008. Contradictions and justifications: Extensions to the textual entailment task.

Jonathan Weese, Juri Ganitkevitch, Chris Callison-Burch, Matt Post, and Adam Lopez. 2011. Joshua 3.0: Syntax-based machine translation with the thrax grammar extractor. EMNLP 2011 - Workshop on statistical machine translation.

Shiqi Zhao, Cheng Niu, Ming Zhou, Ting Liu, and Sheng Li. 2008. Combining multiple resources to improve SMT-based paraphrasing model. In *Proceedings of ACL/HLT.*

Andreas Zollmann and Ashish Venugopal. 2006. Syntax augmented machine translation via chart parsing. In *Proceedings of WMT06.*

Encoding syntactic dependencies by vector permutation

Pierpaolo Basile
Dept. of Computer Science
University of Bari
Via Orabona, 4
I-70125, Bari (ITALY)
basilepp@di.uniba.it

Annalina Caputo
Dept. of Computer Science
University of Bari
Via Orabona, 4
I-70125, Bari (ITALY)
acaputo@di.uniba.it

Giovanni Semeraro
Dept. of Computer Science
University of Bari
Via Orabona, 4
I-70125, Bari (ITALY)
semeraro@di.uniba.it

Abstract

Distributional approaches are based on a simple hypothesis: the meaning of a word can be inferred from its usage. The application of that idea to the vector space model makes possible the construction of a WordSpace in which words are represented by mathematical points in a geometric space. Similar words are represented close in this space and the definition of "word usage" depends on the definition of the context used to build the space, which can be the whole document, the sentence in which the word occurs, a fixed window of words, or a specific syntactic context. However, in its original formulation WordSpace can take into account only one definition of context at a time. We propose an approach based on vector permutation and Random Indexing to encode several syntactic contexts in a single WordSpace. Moreover, we propose some operations in this space and report the results of an evaluation performed using the GEMS 2011 Shared Evaluation data.

1 Background and motivation

Distributional approaches usually rely on the WordSpace model (Schütze, 1993). An overview can be found in (Sahlgren, 2006). This model is based on a vector space in which points are used to represent semantic concepts, such as words.

The core idea behind WordSpace is that words and concepts are represented by points in a mathematical space, and this representation is learned from text in such a way that concepts with similar or related meanings are near to one another in that space (geometric metaphor of meaning). The semantic similarity between concepts can be represented as proximity in an n-dimensional space. Therefore, the main feature of the geometric metaphor of meaning is not that meanings can be represented as locations in a semantic space, but rather that similarity between word meanings can be expressed in spatial terms, as proximity in a high-dimensional space.

One of the great virtues of WordSpaces is that they make very few language-specific assumptions, since just tokenized text is needed to build semantic spaces. Even more important is their independency of the quality (and the quantity) of available training material, since they can be built by exploiting an entirely unsupervised distributional analysis of free text. Indeed, the basis of the WordSpace model is the *distributional hypothesis* (Harris, 1968), according to which the meaning of a word is determined by the set of textual *contexts* in which it appears. As a consequence, in distributional models words can be represented as vectors built over the observable *contexts*. This means that words are semantically related as much as they are represented by similar vectors. For example, if "basketball" and "tennis" occur frequently in the same context, say after "play", they are semantically related or similar according to the distributional hypothesis.

Since co-occurrence is defined with respect to a context, co-occurring words can be stored into matrices whose rows represent the terms and columns represent contexts. More specifically, each row corresponds to a vector representation of a word. The strength of the semantic association between words can be computed by using cosine similarity.

A weak point of distributional approaches is that they are able to encode only one definition of context at a time. The type of semantics represented in WordSpace depends on the context. If we choose documents as context we obtain a semantics different from the one we would obtain by selecting sentences as context. Several approaches have investigated the above mentioned problem: (Baroni and Lenci, 2010) use a representation based on third-order tensors and provide a general framework for distributional semantics in which it is possible to represent several aspects of meaning using a single data structure. (Sahlgren et al., 2008) adopt vector permutations as a means to encode order in WordSpace, as described in Section 2. BEAGLE (Jones and Mewhort, 2007) is a very well-known method to encode word order and context information in WordSpace. The drawback of the BEAGLE model is that it relies on a complex model to build vectors which is computational expensive. This problem is solved by (De Vine and Bruza, 2010) in which the authors propose an approach similar to BEAGLE, but using a method based on Circular Holographic Reduced Representations to compute vectors.

All these methods tackle the problem of representing word order in WordSpace, but they do not take into account syntactic context. A valuable attempt in this direction is described in (Padó and Lapata, 2007). In this work, the authors propose a method to build WordSpace using information about syntactic dependencies. In particular, they consider syntactic dependencies as context and assign different weights to each kind of dependency. Moreover, they take into account the distance between two words into the graph of dependencies. The results obtained by the authors support our hypothesis that syntactic information can be useful to produce effective WordSpace. Nonetheless, their methods are not able to directly encode syntactic dependencies into the space.

This work aims to provide a simple approach to encode syntactic relations dependencies directly into the WordSpace, dealing with both the scalability problem and the possibility to encode several context information. To achieve that goal, we developed a strategy based on Random Indexing and vector permutations. Moreover, this strategy opens new possibilities in the area of semantic composition as a result of the inherent capability of encoding relations between words.

The paper is structured as follows. Section 2 describes Random Indexing, the strategy for building our WordSpace, while details about the method used to encode syntactic dependencies are reported in Section 3. Section 4 describes the formal definition of some operations over the WordSpace and shows a first attempt to define a model for semantic composition. Finally, the results of the evaluation performed using the GEMS 2011 Shared Evaluation data[1] is presented in Section 5, while conclusions are reported in Section 6.

2 Random Indexing

We exploit Random Indexing (RI), introduced by Kanerva (Kanerva, 1988), for creating a WordSpace. This technique allows us to build a WordSpace with no need for (either term-document or term-term) matrix factorization, because vectors are inferred by using an incremental strategy. Moreover, it allows to solve efficiently the problem of reducing dimensions, which is one of the key features used to uncover the "latent semantic dimensions" of a word distribution.

RI is based on the concept of Random Projection according to which high dimensional vectors chosen randomly are "nearly orthogonal".

Formally, given an $n \times m$ matrix A and an $m \times k$ matrix R made up of k m-dimensional random vectors, we define a new $n \times k$ matrix B as follows:

$$B^{n,k} = A^{n,m} \cdot R^{m,k} \quad k << m \tag{1}$$

The new matrix B has the property to preserve the distance between points. This property is known as Johnson-Lindenstrauss lemma: if the distance between two any points of A is d, then the distance d_r between the corresponding points in B will satisfy the property that $d_r = c \cdot d$. A proof of that property is reported in (Dasgupta and Gupta, 1999).

Specifically, RI creates a WordSpace in two steps (in this case we consider the document as context):

[1] Available on line:
http://sites.google.com/site/geometricalmodels/shared-evaluation

1. a context vector is assigned to each document. This vector is sparse, high-dimensional and ternary, which means that its elements can take values in {-1, 0, 1}. A context vector contains a small number of randomly distributed non-zero elements, and the structure of this vector follows the hypothesis behind the concept of Random Projection;

2. context vectors are accumulated by analyzing terms and documents in which terms occur. In particular, the semantic vector for a term is computed as the sum of the context vectors for the documents which contain that term. Context vectors are multiplied by term occurrences.

Formally, given a collection of documents D whose vocabulary of terms is V (we denote with $dim(D)$ and $dim(V)$ the dimension of D and V, respectively) the above steps can be formalized as follows:

1. $\forall d_i \in D$, $i = 0, .., dim(D)$ we built the correspondent randomly generated context vector as:

$$\overrightarrow{r_j} = (r_{i1}, ..., r_{in}) \tag{2}$$

   where $n \ll \dim(D)$, $r_{i*} \in \{-1, 0, 1\}$ and $\overrightarrow{r_j}$ contains only a small number of elements different from zero;

2. the WordSpace is made up of all term vectors $\overrightarrow{t_j}$ where:

$$\overrightarrow{t_j} = tf_j \sum_{\substack{d_i \in D \\ t_j \in d_i}} \overrightarrow{r_i} \tag{3}$$

   and tf_j is the number of occurrences of t_j in d_i;

By considering a fixed window W of terms as context, the WordSpace is built as follows:

1. a context vector is assigned to each term;

2. context vectors are accumulated by analyzing terms in which terms co-occur in a window W. In particular, the semantic vector for each term is computed as the sum of the context vectors for terms which co-occur in W.

It is important to point out that the classical RI approach can handle only one context at a time, such as the whole document or the window W.

A method to add information about context in RI is proposed in (Sahlgren et al., 2008). The authors describe a strategy to encode word order in RI by the permutation of coordinates in random vector. When the coordinates are shuffled using a random permutation, the resulting vector is nearly orthogonal to the original one. That operation corresponds to the generation of a new random vector. Moreover, by applying a predetermined mechanism to obtain random permutations, such as elements rotation, it is always possible to reconstruct the original vector using the reverse permutations. By exploiting this strategy it is possible to obtain different random vectors for each context[2] in which the term occurs. Let us consider the following example "The cat eats the mouse". To encode the word order for the word "cat" using a context window $W = 3$, we obtain:

$$\begin{aligned} < cat >= (\Pi^{-1} the) + (\Pi^{+1} eat) + \\ +(\Pi^{+2} the) + (\Pi^{+3} mouse) \end{aligned} \tag{4}$$

where $\Pi^n x$ indicates a rotation by n places of the elements in the vector x. Indeed, the rotation is performed by n right-shifting steps.

3 Encoding syntactic dependencies

Our idea is to encode syntactic dependencies, instead of words order, in the WordSpace using vector permutations.

A syntactic dependency between two words is defined as:

$$dep(head, dependent) \tag{5}$$

where dep is the syntactic link which connects the $dependent$ word to the $head$ word. Generally speaking, $dependent$ is the modifier, object or complement, while $head$ plays a key role in determining the behavior of the link. For example, $subj(eat, cat)$ means that "cat" is the subject of "eat". In that case the $head$ word is "eat", which plays the role of verb.

The key idea is to assign a permutation function to each kind of syntactic dependencies. Formally,

[2]In the case in point the context corresponds to the word order

let D be the set of all dependencies that we take into account. The function $f : D \rightarrow \Pi$ returns a schema of vector permutation for each $dep \in D$. Then, the method adopted to construct a semantic space that takes into account both syntactic dependencies and Random Indexing can be defined as follows:

1. a context vector is assigned to each term, as described in Section 2 (Random Indexing);
2. context vectors are accumulated by analyzing terms which are linked by a dependency. In particular the semantic vector for each term t_i is computed as the sum of the permuted context vectors for the terms t_j which are dependents of t_i and the inverse-permuted vectors for the terms t_j which are heads of t_i. The permutation is computed according to f. If $f(d) = \Pi^n$ the inverse-permutation is defined as $f^{-1}(d) = \Pi^{-n}$: the elements rotation is performed by n left-shifting steps.

Adding permuted vectors to the head word and inverse-permuted vectors to the corresponding dependent word allows to encode the information about both heads and dependents into the space. This approach is similar to the one investigated by (Cohen et al., 2010) to encode relations between medical terms.

To clarify, we provide an example. Given the following definition of f:

$$f(subj) = \Pi^{+3} \qquad f(obj) = \Pi^{+7} \tag{6}$$

and the sentence "The cat eats the mouse", we obtain the following dependencies:

$$\begin{array}{cc} det(the, cat) & subj(eat, cat) \\ obj(eat, mouse) & det(the, mouse) \end{array} \tag{7}$$

The semantic vector for each word is computed as:

- *eat*:
$$< eat >= (\Pi^{+3}cat) + (\Pi^{+7}mouse) \tag{8}$$
- *cat*:
$$< cat >= (\Pi^{-3}eat) \tag{9}$$
- *mouse*:
$$< mouse >= (\Pi^{-7}eat) \tag{10}$$

In the above examples, the function f does not consider the dependency det.

4 Query and vector operations

In this section, we propose two types of queries that allow us to compute semantic similarity between two words exploiting syntactic dependencies encoded in our space. Before defining query and vector operations, we introduce a small set of notations:

- R denotes the original space of random vectors generated during the WordSpace construction;
- S is the space of terms built using our strategy;
- $r_{t_i} \in R$ denotes the random vector of the term t_i;
- $s_{t_i} \in S$ denotes the semantic vector of the term t_i;
- $sim(v_1, v_2)$ denotes the similarity between two vectors; in our approach we adopt cosine similarity;
- Π^{dep} is the permutation returned from $f(dep)$. Π^{-dep} is the inverse-permutation.

The first family of queries is $dep(t_i, ?)$. The idea is to find all the dependents which are in relation with the $head$ t_i, given the dependency dep. The query can be computed as follows:

1. retrieve the vector s_{t_i} from S;
2. for each $r_{t_j} \in R$ compute the similarity between s_{t_i} and $< \Pi^{dep} r_{t_j} >$:
$$sim(s_{t_i}, < \Pi^{dep} r_{t_j} >);$$
3. rank in descending order all t_j according to the similarity computed in step 2.

The idea behind this operation is to compute how each possible dependent t_j contributes to the vector t_i, which is the sum of all the dependents related to t_i. It is important to note that we must first apply the permutation to each r_{t_j} in order to take into account the dependency relation (context). This operation has a semantics different from performing the query by applying first the inverse permutation to t_i in R and then computing the similarity with respect to all the vectors t_j in S. Indeed, the last approach would compute how the head t_i contributes to the vector t_j, which differs from the goal of our query.

Using the same approach it is possible to compute the query $dep(?, t_j)$, in which we want to search all the $heads$ related to the $dependent$ t_j fixed the dependency dep. In detail:

1. retrieve the vector s_{t_j} from S;
2. for each $r_{t_i} \in R$ compute the similarity between s_{t_j} and the inverse-permutation of r_{t_i}, $< \Pi^{-dep} r_{t_i} >$: $sim(s_{t_j}, < \Pi^{-dep} r_{t_i} >)$;
3. rank in descending order all t_i according to the similarity computed in step 2.

In this second query, we compute how the inverse-permutation of each t_i (head) affects the vector $s_{t_j} \in S$. In the following sub-section we provide some initial idea about semantic composition.

4.1 Compositional semantics

Distributional approaches represent words in isolation and they are typically used to compute similarities between words. They are not able to represent complex structures such as phrases or sentences. In some applications, such as Question Answering and Text Entailment, representing text by single words is not enough. These applications would benefit from the composition of words in more complex structures. The strength of our approach lies on the capability of codify syntactic relations between words overcoming the "word isolation" issue.

A lot of recent work argue that tensor product ($\otimes$) could be useful to combine word vectors. In (Widdows, 2008) some preliminary investigations about product and tensor product are provided, while an interesting work by Clark and Pulman (Clark and Pulman, 2007) proposes an approach to combine symbolic and distributional models. The main idea is to use tensor product to combine these two aspects, but the authors do not describe a method to represent symbolic features, such as syntactic dependencies. Conversely, our approach is able to encode syntactic information directly into the distributional model. The authors in (Clark and Pulman, 2007) propose a strategy to represent a sentence like "man reads magazine" by tensor product:

$$man \otimes subj \otimes read \otimes obj \otimes magazine \quad (11)$$

They also propose a solid model for compositionality, but they do not provide a strategy to represent symbolic relations, such as $subj$ and obj. They wrote: "How to obtain vectors for the dependency relations - subj, obj, etc. - is an open question". We believe that our approach can tackle this problem by encoding the dependency directly in the space, because each semantic vector in our space contains information about syntactic roles.

The representation based on tensor product is useful to compute sentence similarity. Given the previous sentence and the following one "woman browses newspaper", we want to compute the similarity between the two sentences. The sentence "woman browses newspaper", using the compositional model, is represented by:

$$woman \otimes subj \otimes browse \otimes obj \otimes newspaper \quad (12)$$

Computing the similarity of two representations by inner product is a complex task, but exploiting the following property of the tensor product:

$$(w_1 \otimes w_2) \cdot (w_3 \otimes w_4) = (w_1 \cdot w_3) \times (w_2 \cdot w_4) \quad (13)$$

the similarity between two sentences can be computed by taking into account the pairs in each dependency and multiplying the inner products as follows:

$$\begin{aligned} man \cdot woman \times read \cdot browse \times \\ \times magazine \cdot newspaper \end{aligned} \quad (14)$$

According to the property above mentioned, we can compute the similarity between sentences without using the tensor product. However, some open questions arise. This simple compositional strategy allows to compare sentences which have similar dependency trees. For example, the sentence "the dog bit the man" cannot can be compared to "the man was bitten by the dog". This problem can be easily solved by identifying active and passive forms of a verb. When two sentences have different trees, Clark and Pulman (Clark and Pulman, 2007) propose to adopt the *convolution kernel* (Haussler, 1999). This strategy identifies all the possible ways of decomposing the two trees, and sums up the similarities between all the pairwise decompositions. It is important to point out that, in a more recent work, Clark et al. (Clark et al., 2008) propose a model based on (Clark and Pulman, 2007) combined with a compositional theory for grammatical types, known as Lambek's pregroup semantics, which is able to take into account grammar structures. It is important to note that this strategy is not able to encode grammatical roles into the WordSpace. This peculiarity makes our approach completely different. In the following section we provide some examples of compositionality.

5 Evaluation

The goal of the evaluation is twofold: proving the capability of our approach by means of some examples and providing results of the evaluation exploiting the "GEMS 2011 Shared Evaluation", in particular the compositional semantics dataset. We propose two semantic spaces built from two separate corpora using our strategy. To achieve the first goal we provide several examples for each family of queries described in Section 4. Concerning the second goal, we evaluate our approach to compositional semantics using the dataset proposed by Mitchell and Lapata (Mitchell and Lapata, 2010), which is part of the "GEMS 2011 Shared Evaluation". The dataset is a list of two pairs of adjective-noun combinations or verb-object combinations or compound nouns. Humans rated pairs of combinations according to similarity. The dataset contains 5,833 rates which range from 1 to 7. Examples of pairs follow:

support offer help provide 7

old person right hand 1

where the similarity between offer-support and provide-help (verb-object) is higher than the one between old-person and right-hand (adjective-noun). As suggested by the authors, the goal of the evaluation is to compare the system performace against humans scores by means of Spearman correlation.

5.1 System setup

The system is implemented in Java and relies on some portions of code publicly available in the Semantic Vectors package (Widdows and Ferraro, 2008). For the evaluation of the system, we build two separate WordSpaces using the following corpora: ukWaC (Baroni et al., 2009) and TASA. ukWaC contains 2 billion words and it is constructed from the Web by limiting the crawling to the .uk domain and using medium-frequency words from the BNC corpus as seeds. We use only a portion of ukWaC corpus consisting of 7,025,587 sentences (about 220,000 documents). The TASA corpus (compiled by Touchstone Applied Science Associates) was kindly made available to us by Prof. Thomas Landauer from the University of Colorado. The TASA corpus contains a collection of English texts that is approximately equivalent to what the average college-level student has read in his/her lifetime. The TASA corpus consists of about 800,000 sentences.

To extract syntactic dependencies, we adopt MINIPAR[3] (Lin, 2003). MINIPAR is an efficient English parser, which is suitable for parsing a large amount of data. The total amount of extracted dependencies is about 112,500,000 for ukWaC and 8,850,000 for TASA.

Our approach involves some parameters. We set the random vector dimension to 4,000 and the number of non-zero elements in the random vector equal to 10. We restrict the WordSpace to the 40,000 most frequent words[4]. Another parameter is the set of dependencies that we take into account. In this preliminary investigation we consider the four dependencies described in Table 1, that reports also the kind of permutation[5] applied to vectors.

5.2 Results

In this section we report some results of queries performed in ukWaC and TASA corpus.

Table 2 and Table 3 report the results respectively for the queries $dep(t_i, ?)$ and $dep(?, t_j)$. The effects of encoding syntactic information is clearly visible, as can be inferred by results in the tables. Moreover, the results with the two corpora are different, as expected, but in many cases the first result of the query is the same.

Our space can be also exploited to perform classical queries in which we want to find "similar" words. Tables 4 and 5 report results for TASA and ukWaC

[3]MINIPAR is available at http://webdocs.cs.ualberta.ca/~lindek/minipar.htm

[4]Word frequency is computed taking into account the selected dependencies.

[5]The number of rotations is randomly chosen.

Dependency	Description	Permutation
obj	object of verbs	Π^{+7}
subj	subject of verbs	Π^{+3}
mod	the relationship between a word and its adjunct modifier	Π^{+11}
comp	complement	Π^{+23}

Table 1: The set of dependencies used in the evaluation.

corpus, respectively. The results obtained by similar test are not the typical results expected by classical WordSpace. In fact, in Table 5 the word most similar to "good" is "bad", because they are used in the same syntactic context, but have opposite meaning. The similarity between words in our space strongly depends on their syntactic role. For example, the words similar to "food" are all the nouns which are object/subject of the same verbs in syntactic relation with "food".

Finally, we provide the results of semantic composition. Table 6 reports the Spearman correlation between the output of our system and the mean similarity scores given by the humans. The table shows results for each types of combination: verb-object, adjective-noun and compound nouns. To perform the experiment on compound nouns, we rebuild the spaces encoding the "nn" relation provided by MINIPAR which refers to compound nouns dependency. Table 6 shows the best result obtained by Mitchell and Lapata (Mitchell and Lapata, 2008) using the same dataset. Our method is able to outperform ML_{best} and obtains very high results when adjective-noun combination is involved.

Corpus	Combination	ρ
TASA	verb-object	0.260
	adjective-noun	0.637
	compound nouns	0.341
	overall	**0.275**
ukWaC	verb-object	0.292
	adjective-noun	0.445
	compound nouns	0.227
	overall	**0.261**
-	ML_{best}	*0.190*

Table 6: GEMS 2011 Shared Evaluation results.

The experiments reported in this preliminary evaluation are only a small fraction of the experiments that are required to make a proper evaluation of the effectiveness of our semantic space and to compare it with other approaches. This will be the main focus of our future research. The obtained results seem to be encouraging and the strength of our approach, capturing syntactic relations, allows to implement several kind of queries using only one WordSpace. We believe that the real advantage of our approach, that is the possibility to represent several syntactic relations, has much room for exploration.

6 Conclusions

In this work, we propose an approach to encode syntactic dependencies in WordSpace using vector permutations and Random Indexing. In that space, a set of operations is defined, which relies on the possibility of exploiting syntactic dependencies to perform some particular queries, such as the one for retrieving all similar objects of a verb. We propose an early attempt to use that space for semantic composition of short sentences. The evaluation using the GEMS 2011 shared dataset provides encouraging results, but we believe that there are open points which deserve more investigation. We planned a deeper evaluation of our WordSpace and a more formal study about semantic composition.

Acknowledgements

This research was partially funded by MIUR (Ministero dell'Università e della Ricerca) under the contract Fondo per le Agevolazioni alla Ricerca, DM19410 "Laboratorio" di Bioinformatica per la Biodiversità Molecolare (2007-2011).

$obj(provide, ?)$				$mod(people, ?)$			
TASA		ukWaC		TASA		ukWaC	
information	0.344	information	0.351	young	0.288	young	0.736
food	0.208	service	0.260	black	0.118	with	0.360
support	0.143	you	0.176	old	0.089	other	0.223
energy	0.143	opportunity	0.141	conquered	0.086	handling	0.164
job	0.142	support	0.127	deaf	0.086	impressive	0.162

Table 2: Examples of query $dep(t_i, ?)$.

$obj(?, food)$				$mod(?, good)$			
TASA		ukWaC		TASA		ukWaC	
eat	0.604	eat	0.429	idea	0.350	practice	0.510
make	0.389	serve	0.256	place	0.320	idea	0.363
grow	0.311	provide	0.230	way	0.269	news	0.274
need	0.272	have	0.177	friend	0.246	for	0.269
store	0.161	buy	0.169	time	0.234	very	0.228

Table 3: Examples of query $dep(?, t_j)$.

food		provide		good	
food	1.000	provide	1.000	good	0.999
foods	0.698	make	0.702	best	0.498
meat	0.654	restructure	0.693	excellent	0.471
meal	0.651	ready	0.680	wrong	0.453
bread	0.606	leave	0.673	main	0.430
wheato	0.604	mean	0.672	nice	0.428
thirty_percent	0.604	work	0.672	safe	0.428
mezas	0.604	offer	0.671	new	0.428
orgy	0.604	relate	0.667	proper	0.400
chocolatebar	0.604	gather	0.667	surrounded	0.400

Table 4: Find similar words, TASA corpus.

food		provide		good	
food	1.000	provide	0.999	good	1.000
meal	0.724	offer	0.855	bad	0.603
meat	0.656	supply	0.819	best	0.545
pie	0.578	deliver	0.801	anti-discriminatory	0.507
tea	0.576	give	0.787	nice	0.478
fresh_food	0.576	contain	0.786	reflective	0.470
supper	0.556	require	0.784	brilliant	0.464
porridge	0.553	present	0.782	great	0.462
entertainment	0.533	gather	0.778	evidence-based	0.453
soup	0.532	work	0.777	unsafe	0.444

Table 5: Find similar words, ukWaC corpus.

References

M. Baroni and A. Lenci. 2010. Distributional memory: A general framework for corpus-based semantics. *Computational Linguistics*, 36(4):673–721.

M. Baroni, S. Bernardini, A. Ferraresi, and E. Zanchetta. 2009. The WaCky Wide Web: A collection of very large linguistically processed Web-crawled corpora. *Language Resources and Evaluation*, 43(3):209–226.

S. Clark and S. Pulman. 2007. Combining symbolic and distributional models of meaning. In *Proceedings of the AAAI Spring Symposium on Quantum Interaction*, pages 52–55.

S. Clark, B. Coecke, and M. Sadrzadeh. 2008. A compositional distributional model of meaning. In *Proceedings of the Second Quantum Interaction Symposium (QI-2008)*, pages 133–140.

T. Cohen, D. Widdows, R.W. Schvaneveldt, and T.C. Rindflesch. 2010. Logical leaps and quantum connectives: Forging paths through predication space. In *AAAI-Fall 2010 Symposium on Quantum Informatics for Cognitive, Social, and Semantic Processes*, pages 11–13.

S. Dasgupta and A. Gupta. 1999. An elementary proof of the Johnson-Lindenstrauss lemma. Technical report, Technical Report TR-99-006, International Computer Science Institute, Berkeley, California, USA.

L. De Vine and P. Bruza. 2010. Semantic Oscillations: Encoding Context and Structure in Complex Valued Holographic Vectors. *Quantum Informatics for Cognitive, Social, and Semantic Processes (QI 2010)*.

Z. Harris. 1968. *Mathematical Structures of Language*. New York: Interscience.

D. Haussler. 1999. Convolution kernels on discrete structures. *Technical Report UCSC-CRL-99-10*.

M.N. Jones and D.J.K. Mewhort. 2007. Representing word meaning and order information in a composite holographic lexicon. *Psychological review*, 114(1):1–37.

P. Kanerva. 1988. *Sparse Distributed Memory*. MIT Press.

D. Lin. 2003. Dependency-based evaluation of MINIPAR. *Treebanks: building and using parsed corpora*.

J. Mitchell and M. Lapata. 2008. Vector-based models of semantic composition. In *Proceedings of ACL-08: HLT*, pages 236–244, Columbus, Ohio, June. Association for Computational Linguistics.

J. Mitchell and M. Lapata. 2010. Composition in distributional models of semantics. *Cognitive Science*. To appear.

S. Padó and M. Lapata. 2007. Dependency-based construction of semantic space models. *Computational Linguistics*, 33(2):161–199.

M. Sahlgren, A. Holst, and P. Kanerva. 2008. Permutations as a means to encode order in word space. In *Proceedings of the 30th Annual Meeting of the Cognitive Science Society (CogSci'08)*.

M. Sahlgren. 2006. *The Word-Space Model: Using distributional analysis to represent syntagmatic and paradigmatic relations between words in high-dimensional vector spaces*. Ph.D. thesis, Stockholm: Stockholm University, Faculty of Humanities, Department of Linguistics.

H. Schütze. 1993. Word space. In Stephen José Hanson, Jack D. Cowan, and C. Lee Giles, editors, *Advances in Neural Information Processing Systems*, pages 895–902. Morgan Kaufmann Publishers.

D. Widdows and K. Ferraro. 2008. Semantic Vectors: A Scalable Open Source Package and Online Technology Management Application. In *Proceedings of the 6th International Conference on Language Resources and Evaluation (LREC 2008)*.

D. Widdows. 2008. Semantic vector products: Some initial investigations. In *The Second AAAI Symposium on Quantum Interaction*.

Assessing Interpretable, Attribute-related Meaning Representations for Adjective-Noun Phrases in a Similarity Prediction Task

Matthias Hartung and **Anette Frank**
Computational Linguistics Department
Heidelberg University
{hartung, frank}@cl.uni-heidelberg.de

Abstract

We present a distributional vector space model that incorporates Latent Dirichlet Allocation in order to capture the semantic relation holding between adjectives and nouns along interpretable dimensions of meaning: The meaning of adjective-noun phrases is characterized in terms of ontological attributes that are prominent in their compositional semantics. The model is evaluated in a similarity prediction task based on paired adjective-noun phrases from the Mitchell and Lapata (2010) benchmark data. Comparing our model against a high-dimensional latent word space, we observe qualitative differences that shed light on different aspects of similarity conveyed by both models and suggest integrating their complementary strengths.

1 Introduction

This paper offers a comparative evaluation of two types of accounts to the compositional meaning of adjective-noun phrases. This comparison is embedded in a similarity judgement task that determines the semantic similarity of pairs of adjective-noun phrases. All models we consider establish the similarity of adjective-noun pairs by measuring similarity between vectors representing the meaning of the individual adjective-noun phrases. However, the models we investigate differ in the type of interpretation they assign to adjectives, nouns and the phrases composed from them.

One type of approach is represented by the classical vector space model (VSM) of Mitchell and Lapata (2010; henceforth: M&L). It represents the semantics of adjective-noun phrases in *latent semantic space*, based on dimensions defined by bags of context words. This classical model will be compared against a compositional analysis of adjective-noun phrases that represents adjectives and nouns along *interpretable dimensions* of meaning, i.e. discrete ontological attributes such as SIZE, COLOR, SPEED, WEIGHT. Here, lexical vectors for adjectives and nouns define possible attribute meanings as component values; vector composition is intended to elicit those attributes that are prominent in the meaning of the whole phrase. For instance, a composed vector representation of the phrase *hot pepper* is expected to yield high component values on the dimensions TASTE and SMELL, rather than TEMPERATURE. The underlying relations between adjectives and nouns, respectively, and the attributes they denote is captured by way of latent semantic information obtained from Latent Dirichlet Allocation (LDA; Blei et al. (2003)). Thus, we treat attributes as an abstract meaning layer that generalizes over latent topics inferred by LDA and utilize this interpretable layer as the dimensions of our VSM.

This approach has been shown to be effective in an *attribute selection* task (Hartung and Frank, 2011), where the goal is to predict the most prominent attribute(s) "hidden" in the compositional semantics of adjective-noun phrases. In this paper, our main interest is to assess the potential of modeling adjective semantics in terms of discrete, interpretable attribute meanings in a similarity judgement task, as opposed to a representation in latent semantic space that is usually applied to tasks of this kind.

For this purpose, we rely on the evaluation data set of M&L which serves as a shared benchmark in the GEMS 2011 workshop. Their similarity judgement task, being tailored to measuring latent similarity, represents a true challenge for an analysis focused on discrete ontological attributes.

Our results show that the latent semantic model of M&L cannot be beaten by an interpreted analysis based on LDA topic models. However, we show substantial performance improvements of the interpreted analysis in specific settings with adapted training and test sets that enable focused comparison. An interesting outcome of our investigations is that – using an interpreted LDA analysis of adjective-noun phrases – we uncover divergences in the notions of similarity underlying the judgement task that go virtually unnoticed in a latent semantic VSM, while they need to be clearly distinguished in models focused on interpretable representations.

The paper is structured as follows: After a brief summarization of related work, Section 3 introduces *Controled LDA*, a weakly supervised extension to standard LDA, and explains how it can be utilized to inject interpretable meaning dimensions into VSMs. In Section 4, we describe the parameters and experimental settings for comparing our model to M&L's word-based latent VSM in a similarity prediction task. Section 5 presents the results of this experiment, followed by a thorough qualitative analysis of the specific strengths and weaknesses of both models in Section 6. Section 7 concludes.

2 Related Work

Recent work in distributional semantics has engendered different perspectives on how to characterize the semantics of adjectives and adjective-noun phrases.

Almuhareb (2006) aims at capturing the semantics of adjectives in terms of attributes they denote using lexico-syntactic patterns. His approach suffers from severe sparsity problems and does not account for the compositional nature of adjective-noun phrases, as it disregards the meaning contributed by the noun. It is therefore unable to perform disambiguation of adjectives in the context of a noun.

Baroni and Zamparelli (2010) and Guevara (2010) focus on how best to represent compositionality in adjective-noun phrases considering different types of composition operators. These works adhere to a fully latent representation of meaning, whereas Hartung and Frank (2010) assign symbolic attribute meanings to adjectives, nouns and composed phrases by incorporating attributes as dimensions in a compositional VSM. By holding the attribute meaning of adjectives and nouns in distinct vector representations and combining them through vector composition, their approach improves on both weaknesses of Almuhareb's work. However, their account is still closely tied to Almuhareb's pattern-based approach in that counts of co-occurrence patterns linking adjectives and nouns to attributes are used to populate the vector representations. These, however, are inherently sparse. The resulting model therefore still suffers from sparsity of co-occurrence data.

Finally, Latent Dirichlet Allocation, originally designed for tasks such as text classification and document modeling (Blei et al., 2003), found its way into lexical semantics. Ritter et al. (2010) and Ó Séaghdha (2010), e.g., model selectional restrictions of verb arguments by inducing topic distributions that characterize mixtures of topics observed in verb argument positions. Mitchell and Lapata (2009, 2010) were the first to use LDA-inferred topics as dimensions in VSMs.

Hartung and Frank (2011) adopt a similar approach, by embedding LDA into a VSM for adjective-noun meaning composition, with LDA topics providing latent variables for attribute meanings. That is, contrary to M&L, LDA is used to convey information about interpretable semantic attributes rather than latent topics. In fact, Hartung and Frank (2011) are able to show that "injecting" topic distributions inferred from LDA into a VSM alleviates sparsity problems that persisted with the pattern-based VSM of Hartung and Frank (2010).

Baroni et al. (2010) highlight two strengths of VSMs that incorporate interpretable dimensions of meaning: cognitive plausibility and effectiveness in concept categorization tasks. In their model, concepts are characterized in terms of salient properties and relations (e.g., *children* have *parents*, *grass* is *green*). However, their approach concentrates on nouns. Open questions are (i) whether it can be extended to further word classes, and (ii) whether the interpreted meaning layers are interoperable across word classes, to cope with compositionality. The present paper extends their work by offering a test case for an interpretable, compositional VSM, applied to adjective-noun composition with attributes as a shared meaning layer. Moreover, to our knowledge, we are the first to expose such a model to a pairwise similarity judgement task.

3 Attribute Modeling based on LDA

3.1 Controled LDA

This section introduces *Controled LDA* (C-LDA), a weakly supervised variant of LDA. We use C-LDA to model attribute information that pertains to adjectives and nouns individually. This information is "injected" into a vector-space framework as a basis for computing the attributes that are prominent in compositional adjective-noun phrases.

In its original statement, LDA is a fully unsupervised process that estimates topic distributions over documents θ_d and word-topic distributions ϕ_t with topics represented as hidden variables. Estimating these parameters on a document collection yields *topic proportions* $P(t|d)$ and *topic distributions* $P(w|t)$ that can be used to compute a smooth distribution $P(w|d)$ as in (1), where t denotes a latent topic, w a word and d a document in the corpus.

$$P(w|d) = \sum_t P(w|t)P(t|d) \qquad (1)$$

While the generative story underlying both models is identical, C-LDA extends standard LDA by "implicitly" taking supervised category information into account. This allows for linking latent topics to interpretable semantic attributes. The idea is to collect *pseudo-documents* in a controlled way such that each document conveys semantic information about one specific attribute. The pseudo-documents are selected along syntactic dependency paths linking the respective attribute noun to meaningful context words (adjectives and nouns). A corpus consisting of the two sentences in (2), e.g., yields a pseudo-document for the attribute noun SPEED containing *car* and *fast*.

(2) What is the speed of this car? The machine runs at a very fast speed.

Note that, though we are ultimately interested in triples between attributes, adjectives and nouns that are conveyed by the compositional semantics of adjective-noun phrases, C-LDA is only exposed to binary tuples between attributes and adjectives or nouns, respectively. This is in line with the findings of Hartung and Frank (2010), who obtained substantial performance improvements by splitting the triples into separate binary relations.

3.2 Embedding C-LDA into a VSM

The main difference of C-LDA compared to standard LDA is that the estimated topic proportions $P(t|d)$ of the former will be highly attribute-specific, and similarly so for the topic distributions $P(w|t)$. We experiment with two variants of VSMs that differ in the way they integrate attribute information inferred from C-LDA, denoted as C-LDA-A and C-LDA-T.

In C-LDA-A, the dimensions of the space are interpretable attributes. The vector components relating a target word w to an attribute a are set to $P(w|a)$. This probability is obtained from C-LDA by constructing the pseudo-documents as distributional fingerprints of the respective attribute, as described in Section 3.1 above:

$$P(w|a) \approx P(w|d) = \sum_t P(w|t)P(t|d) \qquad (3)$$

C-LDA-T capitalizes on latent topics as dimensions; the vector components are set to the topic proportions $P(w|t)$ as directly obtained from C-LDA.[1]

4 Parameters and Experimental Settings

Data. Our experiments are based on the adjective-noun section of M&L's 2010 evaluation data set[2]. It consists of 108 pairs of adjective-noun phrases that were rated for similarity by human judges.

[1]The "topics as dimensions" approach has also been used by Mitchell and Lapata (2010) for dimensionality reduction. In their word space model, however, this setting leads to a decrease in performance on adjective-noun phrases. Therefore, we do not compare ourselves to this instantiation of their model in this paper.

[2]Available from: `http://homepages.inf.ed.ac.uk/s0453356/share`

Models. We contrast the two LDA-based models (i, ii) C-LDA-A and C-LDA-T with two standard VSMs: (iii) a re-implementation of the latent VSM of M&L and (iv) a dependency-based VSM (DepVSM) which relies on dependency paths that connect the target elements and attribute nouns in local contexts. The paths are identical to the ones used for constructing pseudo-documents in (i) and (ii). Thus, DepVSM relies on the same information as C-LDA-A and C-LDA-T, without capitalizing on the smoothing power provided by LDA.

In the C-LDA models, we experiment with several topic number settings. Depending on the number of attributes $|A|$ contained in the training material (see below), we train one model instance for each topic number in the range from $0.5 \cdot |A|$ to $2 \cdot |A|$. For our LDA implementations, we use MALLET (McCallum, 2002). We run 1000 iterations of Gibbs sampling with hyperparameters set to the default values.

Training data. For C-LDA-A, C-LDA-T and DepVSM we apply two different training scenarios: In the first setting, we collect pseudo-documents instantiating 262 attribute nouns that are linked to adjectives by an `attribute` relation in WordNet (Fellbaum, 1998). The topic distributions induced from this data cover the broadest space of attribute meanings we could produce from WordNet[3]. In a second setting, we assume the presence of an "oracle" that confines the training data to a subset of 33 attribute nouns that are linked to those adjectives that actually occur in the M&L test set, to allow for a focused evaluation. In both C-LDA variants, all adjectives and nouns occurring at least five times in the pseudo-documents become target elements in the VSM. The pseudo-documents are collected along dependency paths extracted from section 2 of the pukWaC corpus (Baroni et al., 2009). The same settings are used for training the DepVSM model.

As the M&L model is not intended to reflect attribute meaning, the training data for this model remains constant. Like M&L, we set the target elements of this model to all types contained in the complete evaluation data set (including nouns, adjectives and verbs) and select the 2000 context words that co-occur most frequently with these targets in pukWaC_2 as the dimensions of the space.

Filters on test set. Given the different types of "semantic gist" of the models described above, we expect that the LDA models perform best on those test pairs that involve attributes known to the model. To test this expectation, we compile a restricted test set containing 43 pairs $(adj_1\ n_1,\ adj_2\ n_2)$ where both adj_1 and adj_2 bear an attribute meaning according to WordNet.

Composition operators. In our experiments, we use a subset of the operators proposed by Mitchell and Lapata (2010) to obtain a compositional representation of adjective-noun phrases from individual vectors: vector multiplication ($\times$; best operator in M&L's experiments on adjective-noun phrases) and vector addition ($+$). Besides, in order to assess the contribution of individual vectors in the composition process, we experiment with two "composition surrogates" by taking the individual adjective (ADJ-only) or noun vector (N-only) as the result of the composition process.

Evaluating the models. The models described above are evaluated against the human similarity judgements data provided by Mitchell and Lapata (2010) as follows: We compute the cosine similarity between the composed vectors representing the adjective-noun phrases in each test pair. Next, we measure the correlation between the model scores and the human judgements in terms of Spearman's ρ, where each human rating is treated as an individual data point. The correlation coefficient finally reported is the average over all instances[4] of one model. For completeness, we also report the correlation score of the best model instance and the standard deviation over all model instances.

5 Discussion of Results

Results on complete test set. Table 1 displays the results achieved by the VSMs based on C-LDA and

[3]Note that in Hartung and Frank (2011) only a subset of these attributes, mainly those characterized as *properties* in WordNet, could be successfully modeled, at overall moderate performance levels.

[4]In fact, only those model instances resulting in a significant correlation with the human judgements ($p < 0.05$) are taken into account. This way, we eliminate both inefficient and overly optimistic model instances.

		+			×			ADJ-only			N-only		
		avg	best	σ	avg	best	σ	avg	best	σ	avg	best	σ
262 attrs	C-LDA-A	0.19	0.25	0.05	0.15	0.20	0.04	0.17	0.23	0.04	0.11	0.23	0.06
	C-LDA-T	0.19	0.24	0.02	**0.28**	0.31	0.02	0.20	0.24	0.02	0.18	0.24	0.03
	M&L	0.21			**0.34**			0.19			**0.27**		
	DepVSM	-0.09			-0.09			-0.14			-0.08		
33 attrs	C-LDA-A	**0.23**	0.27	0.02	0.21	0.24	0.01	**0.27**	0.29	0.01	0.17	0.22	0.02
	C-LDA-T	0.21	0.28	0.03	0.14	0.23	0.04	0.22	0.27	0.03	0.10	0.21	0.06
	M&L	0.21			**0.34**			0.19			**0.27**		
	DepVSM	0.21			0.20			**0.27**			0.19		

Table 1: Correlation coefficients (Spearman's ρ) for different training sets, complete test set

		+			×			ADJ-only			N-only		
		avg	best	σ	avg	best	σ	avg	best	σ	avg	best	σ
262 attrs (filtered)	C-LDA-A	0.22	0.31	0.07	0.12	0.30	0.11	0.18	0.30	0.08	0.17	0.28	0.07
	C-LDA-T	0.25	0.30	0.03	0.26	0.35	0.04	0.24	0.29	0.04	0.19	0.23	0.04
	M&L	**0.38**			**0.40**			0.24			**0.43**		
	DepVSM	0.08			-0.09			0.06			-0.07		
33 attrs (filtered)	C-LDA-A	0.29	0.32	0.02	0.31	0.36	0.02	0.34	0.38	0.02	0.09	0.18	0.04
	C-LDA-T	0.26	0.36	0.05	0.14	0.30	0.09	0.28	0.38	0.07	0.03	0.18	0.08
	M&L	**0.38**			**0.40**			0.24			**0.43**		
	DepVSM	0.34			0.32			**0.35**			0.19		

Table 2: Correlation coefficients (Spearman's ρ) for different training sets and filtered test sets

the M&L word space model on the full adjective-noun test set. The table is split into an upper and a lower part containing the different results obtained from training on 262 and 33 attributes, respectively. Each multicolumn shows the performance achieved by one of the different composition operators presented in Section 4, as well as results obtained from predicting similarity on the basis of raw adjective (ADJ-only) and noun (N-only) vectors.

First and foremost, we observe best overall performance for the M&L model when combined with multiplicative vector composition ($\rho = 0.34$), even though the best results for this setting reported in M&L (2010) ($\rho = 0.46$) cannot be reproduced.

Nevertheless, the C-LDA models show a considerable performance improvement when the training material is constrained to appropriate attributes by an oracle (cf. Sect. 4). Another interesting observation is that the individual adjective and noun vectors produced by M&L and the C-LDA models, respectively, show diametrically opposed performance (cf. 3rd and 4th multicolumn in Table 1).

More in detail, C-LDA-A achieves relative improvements across all composition operators when comparing the 33-ATTR to the 262-ATTR setting. Contrasting C-LDA-A and C-LDA-T, the latter is clearly more effective on the larger training set, especially in combination with the $\times$ operator ($\rho = 0.28$). This might be due to the intersective character of multiplication, which requires densely populated components in both the adjective and the noun vector. This requirement meets best with the C-LDA-T model as long as the number of topics provided is large. The $+$ operator, on the other hand, combines better with C-LDA-A. In the 33-ATTR setting, this combination even outperforms vector addition under the M&L model. Generally, C-LDA-A performs better on the smaller training set, where it leaves C-LDA-T behind in every configuration. This highlights that an interpretable, attribute-related meaning layer generalizing over latent topics can be effective if a small, discriminative set of attributes is available for training. Otherwise, C-LDA-T seems to be more powerful for the present similarity judgement task.

Analyzing the performance of the composition surrogates ADJ-only and N-only in the restricted 33-ATTR setting reveals an interesting twist in the quality of adjective vs. noun vectors: While M&L generally yields better results on noun vectors alone (as compared to adjective vectors), C-LDA-A clearly outperforms M&L in predicting similarity based on adjective meanings in isolation. In this configuration, M&L is also outperformed by the (very strong) dependency baseline which is, in turn, only slightly beaten by C-LDA-A in its best configuration. In fact, it is the ADJ-only surrogate under the C-LDA-A model in its best setting ($\rho = 0.29$) that comes closest to the overall best-performing M&L model. This indicates that modeling attributes in the latent semantics of adjectives can be informative for the present similarity prediction task. The poor quality of the noun vectors, however, limits the overall performance of the C-LDA models considerably.

Results on filtered test set. As can be seen from Table 2, our expectation that C-LDA-A and C-LDA-T should benefit from limiting the test set to instances related to attribute meanings is largely met. We observe overall improvement of correlation scores; also the characteristics of the individual models observed in Table 1 remain unchanged.

However, M&L benefits from filtering as well, and in some configurations, e.g. under vector addition, the relative improvement is even bigger for the latent word space models. This shows that M&L and our C-LDA models are not fully complementary, i.e. some aspects of attribute similarity are also covered by latent models.

Neverthelesss, the adjective/noun twist observed for individual vector performance is corroborated: C-LDA-A's adjective vectors outperform those of M&L by ten points (33 attributes, filtered setting; compared to six points on the complete test set), whereas the performance of the noun vectors drops even further. Again, the DepVSM baseline performs very strong on the adjective vectors in isolation, which clearly underlines that our dependency-based context selection procedure is effective. On the other hand, the individual noun vectors produced by M&L even yield the best overall result on the filtered test data, thus outperforming both composition methods.

Differences in adjective and noun vectors. In order to highlight qualitative differences of the individual adjective and noun vectors across the various models, we analyzed their informativeness in terms of entropy. The intuition is as follows: The lower the entropy exhibited by a vector, the more pronounced are its most prominent components. On the contrary, high entropy indicates a rather broad, less accentuated distribution of the probability mass over the vector components (cf. Hartung and Frank (2010)).

	262 attrs		33 attrs	
	avg	σ	avg	σ
C-LDA-A (JJ)	1.20	0.48	0.83	0.27
C-LDA-A (NN)	1.66	0.72	1.23	0.46
C-LDA-T (JJ)	0.92	0.04	0.50	0.04
C-LDA-T (NN)	1.10	0.06	0.60	0.02
M&L (JJ)	2.74	0.91	2.74	0.91
M&L (NN)	2.96	0.33	2.96	0.33
DepVSM (JJ)	0.48	0.61	0.65	0.32
DepVSM (NN)	0.38	0.67	0.96	0.21

Table 3: Average entropy of individual adjective and noun vectors across different models

The results of this analysis are displayed in Table 3. With regard to the C-LDA models, we observe lower entropy in adjective vectors compared to noun vectors across both training settings, which corresponds to their relative performance in the similarity prediction task. This indicates that C-LDA captures the relation between adjectives and attributes in a very pronounced way, and that this information proves valuable for similarity prediction.

The DepVSM model shows inconsistent results with regard to the different training sets. While the pattern observed for the C-LDA models is confirmed on the limited training set, training on the full set of 262 attributes results in more accentuated noun vectors. Given the huge standard deviations, however, we suppose that these figures are not very reliable.[5]

The correspondence between lower entropy and better performance we could observe for C-LDA-A and C-LDA-T is, however, not confirmed by the M&L word space model, as their adjective vectors exhibit lower entropy on average[6], while they persistently underperform relative to the noun vectors

[5]In fact, unlike the C-LDA models and M&L, DepVSM faces severe sparsity problems on the large training set, as becomes evident from the average total frequency mass per vector: Noun vectors accumulate 704 cooccurrence counts over 262 dimensions on average, while adjective vectors are populated with 1555 counts on average (652 vs. 1052 counts over 33 dimensions on the small training set).

[6]The entropy values of M&L are not directly comparable to those of the C-LDA models and DepVSM; M&L entropies are generally higher due to the higher dimensionality of the model.

(cf. Tables 1 and 2). Note, however, that the entropy values of individual adjective vectors disperse widely around the mean (σ=0.91). This suggests that a considerable proportion of M&L's adjective vectors is rather evenly distributed.

Analyzing the individual performance of noun vectors in terms of entropy is less conclusive. While the noun vectors consistently exhibit relatively high entropy, their varying performance across the different models cannot be explained. We hypothesize that the characteristics of the different models might be more decisive instead: Apparently, attributes as an abstract meaning layer are appropriate for modeling the contribution of adjectives to phrase similarity, whereas the contribution of nouns seems to be captured more effectively by M&L-like distributions along bags of context words.

6 Error Analysis

In order to gain deeper insight into the strengths and weaknesses of C-LDA-A and M&L, we extracted the ten most similar/dissimilar pairs (+Sim/$-$Sim$_{\text{C-LDA-A/M\&L}}$; cf. Table 4) according to system predictions, as well as the ten pairs on which system and human raters show highest/lowest agreement in terms of similarity scores (+Agr/$-$Agr$_{\text{C-LDA-A/M\&L}}$; cf. Table 5), for the best-performing model instance of C-LDA-A and M&L in the unfiltered 33-ATTR setting, respectively.

All pairs in +Sim$_{\text{C-LDA-A}}$ and +Sim$_{\text{M\&L}}$ exhibit matching attributes. +Sim$_{\text{C-LDA-A}}$ contains two pairs involving contrastive attribute values (vs. four in +Sim$_{\text{M\&L}}$): *long period – short time*, *hot weather – cold air*. Obviously, C-LDA-A is not prepared to recognize this type of dissimilarity, as it does not model the semantics and orientation of attribute *values*, and so assigns overly optimistic similarity rates. While this deficiency is explained for C-LDA, it is unexpected for M&L, where in +Sim$_{\text{M\&L}}$ we find pairs such as *old person – elderly lady* with similarity ratings that are almost identical to antonymous pairs discussed above, such as *high price – low cost*.

We further observe a striking difference regarding overall similarity ratings in both systems: We find high scores of 0.88 on average within +Sim$_{\text{C-LDA-A}}$, as opposed to 0.52 in +Sim$_{\text{M\&L}}$. The difference is less marked regarding $-$Sim. Similarly, we find overall low average similarity rates (0.2) in +Agr$_{\text{M\&L}}$, whereas +Agr$_{\text{C-LDA-A}}$ achieves somewhat higher rates (0.27). While all examples point towards dissimilarity, C-LDA-A shows more discriminative power, as exemplified by *hot weather – elderly lady* (lowest rating) vs. *central authority – local office* (highest rating). This suggests that, overall, C-LDA-A disposes of a more discriminative semantic representation to judge similarity – which of course can also go astray.

The disagreement set $-$Agr$_{\text{C-LDA-A}}$ contains the antonymous adjectives with high similarity ratings from +Sim$_{\text{C-LDA-A}}$, of course. We also note a high proportion (5/10) of pairs involving adjectives with vague and highly ambiguous attribute meanings, such as *good, new, certain, general*. These are difficult to capture, especially in combination with abstract noun concepts such as *information, effect* or *circumstance*.

An interesting type of similarity is represented by *early evening – previous day*. In this case, we observe a contrast in the semantics of the nouns involved, while the pair exhibits strong similarity on the attribute level, which is reflected in the system's similarity score. This type of similarity is reminiscent of relational analogies investigated in Turney (2008). A related example is *rural community – federal assembly*. Unlike the human judges, C-LDA predicts high similarity for both pairs.

The examples given in $-$Agr$_{\text{M\&L}}$, by contrast, clearly point to a lack in capturing adjective semantics, with misjudgements such as *effective way – efficient use*, *large number – vast amount* or *large quantity – great majority*.

Turning to $-$Agr$_{\text{C-LDA-A}}$ again, we find 9/10 items exhibit values greater than 0.67 (average: 0.78). This means the model yields a high number of false positives in rating similarity (with explanations and some reservations just discussed). All items in $-$Agr$_{\text{M\&L}}$, by contrast, have values below 0.36 (average: 0.16). That is, we again observe that this model assigns lower similarity scores. This is confirmed by a comparative analysis of average similarity scores on the entire test set: C-LDA-A;+ yields an average similarity of 0.48 (σ=0.05) over all instances, while M&L;$\times$ yields 0.16 on average (σ=0.16). The human ratings (after normalization to the scale from 0 to 1) amount to 0.39 (σ=0.26).

	SIMILARITY			
	C-LDA-A; +		M&L; ×	
+Sim	long period – short time	0.95	important part – significant role	0.66
	hot weather – cold air	0.95	certain circumstance – particular case	0.60
	different kind – various form	0.91	right hand – left arm	0.56
	better job – good place	0.89	long period – short time	0.55
	different part – various form	0.88	old person – elderly lady	0.54
	social event – special circumstance	0.88	high price – low cost	0.54
	better job – good effect	0.88	black hair – dark eye	0.48
	similar result – good effect	0.85	general principle – basic rule	0.44
	social activity – political action	0.82	special circumstance – particular case	0.43
	early evening – previous day	0.80	hot weather – cold air	0.43
−Sim	early stage – long period	0.11	old person – right hand	0.03
	northern region – early age	0.11	new information – further evidence	0.03
	earlier work – early evening	0.11	early stage – dark eye	0.01
	elderly woman – black hair	0.10	practical difficulty – cold air	0.01
	practical difficulty – cold air	0.08	left arm – elderly woman	0.01
	small house – old person	0.07	hot weather – elderly lady	0.00
	left arm – elderly woman	0.06	national government – cold air	0.00
	hot weather – further evidence	0.06	black hair – right hand	0.00
	dark eye – left arm	0.05	hot weather – further evidence	0.00
	national government – cold air	0.03	better job – economic problem	0.00

Table 4: Similarity scores predicted by optimal C-LDA-A and M&L model instances; 33-ATTR setting

	AGREEMENT			
	C-LDA-A; +		M&L; ×	
+Agr	major issue – american country	0.29	similar result – good effect	0.29
	efficient use – little room	0.29	small house – important part	0.14
	economic condition – american country	0.29	national government – new information	0.12
	public building – central authority	0.29	major issue – social event	0.26
	northern region – industrial area	0.28	new body – significant role	0.11
	new life – economic development	0.42	social event – special circumstance	0.25
	new body – significant role	0.13	economic development – rural community	0.32
	hot weather – elderly lady	0.13	new technology – public building	0.18
	social event – low cost	0.13	high price – short time	0.10
	central authority – local office	0.44	new body – whole system	0.24
−Agr	early evening – previous day	0.80	effective way – efficient use	0.29
	rural community – federal assembly	0.67	federal assembly – national government	0.24
	new information – general level	0.68	vast amount – high price	0.10
	similar result – good effect	0.85	different kind – various form	0.24
	better job – good effect	0.88	vast amount – large quantity	0.36
	social event – special circumstance	0.88	large number – vast amount	0.31
	better job – good place	0.89	older man – elderly woman	0.00
	certain circumstance – particular case	0.22	earlier work – early stage	0.00
	hot weather – cold air	0.95	large number – great majority	0.09
	long period – short time	0.95	large quantity – great majority	0.04

Table 5: Test pairs showing high and low agreement between systems and human raters, together with system similarity scores as obtained from optimal model instances; 33-ATTR setting

While these means are not fully comparable as they are the result of different composition operations, the standard deviations suggest that M&L's similarity predictions are dispersed over a larger range of the scale, while the C-LDA scores show only small variation. This missing spread might be one of the reasons for C-LDA's lower performance.

In summary, we note one obvious shortcoming in the C-LDA-A model, in that it does not capture dissimilarity due to distinct contrastive meanings of attribute values in cases of similarity on the noun and attribute levels. With its focus on attribute semantics, however, C-LDA-A is able to capture similarity due to *relational analogies*, as in *early evening – previous day* (0.8), whereas the latent model of M&L is clearly noun-oriented, and thus predicts a low similarity of 0.2 for this pair.

We conclude that the proposed attribute analysis of adjective-noun pairs implements an inherently relational form of similarity. Noun semantics is captured only indirectly, through the range of attributes found relevant for the noun. The current model also fully neglects the meaning of scalar attribute values. Whether a more comprehensive analysis of interpreted adjective-noun meanings is able to succeed in a paired similarity prediction task is an open issue to be explored in future work.

7 Conclusion

In this paper, we presented a distributional VSM that incorporates latent semantic information characterizing ontological attributes in the meaning of adjective-noun phrases, as obtained from C-LDA, a weakly supervised variant of LDA. Originally designed for an attribute selection task (Hartung and Frank, 2011), this model faces a true challenge when evaluated in a pairwise similarity judgement task against a high-dimensional word space model, such as M&L's VSM. In fact, our model is unable to compete with M&L even in its best configurations.

Thorough analysis reveals, however, that the quality of individual adjective and noun vectors is diametric across the two models: C-LDA, capitalizing on interpretable ontological dimensions, produces effective adjective vectors, whereas its noun representations lag behind. The inverse situation is observed for the word-based latent VSM of M&L.

One qualification is in order, though: In its current state, the C-LDA model relies on an "oracle" that pre-selects the attributes involved in the test set for the model to be trained on. Although one could argue that tailoring the context words to the target words has a similar effect in our re-implementation of M&L, interferences of this kind are not desirable in principle. Future work will need to explore in more detail possible attribute ranges with regard to their usefulness for different tasks and data sets.

Our comparative investigaton of the specific strengths and weaknesses of the models indicates that they focus on different aspects of similarity: M&L, possibly due to its higher and more discriminative dimensionality, tends to produce more efficient noun vectors. Overall, this model accords better with human similarity judgements across diverse aspects of similarity than the more focused attribute-oriented LDA models. The C-LDA models focus on a specific, interpretable meaning dimension shared by adjectives and nouns, with a tendency for stronger modeling capacity for adjectives. They are currently not prepared to capture dissimilarity in cases of contrastive attribute values, while on the positive side, they effectively cope with relational analogies, both with similar and dissimilar noun meanings.

Our findings suggest that adding more discriminative power to the noun representations and scalar information about attribute values to the adjective vectors might be beneficial. Further research is needed to investigate how to combine interpretable semantic representations tailored to specific relations, as captured by C-LDA, with M&L-like bag-of-words representations in a single distributional model.

Applying interpreted models to the present similarity rating task will still remain a challenge, as it involves mapping diverse mixtures of aspects and grades of similarity to human judgements. However, if the performance of an integrated model can compete with a purely latent semantic analysis, this offers a clear advantage for more general tasks that require linking phrase meaning to symbolic knowledge bases such as (multilingual) ontologies, or for application scenarios that involve discrete semantic labels, such as text classification based on topic modeling (Blei et al., 2003) or fine-grained named entity classification (Ekbal et al., 2010).

References

Abdulrahman Almuhareb. 2006. *Attributes in Lexical Acquisition*. Ph.D. Dissertation, Department of Computer Science, University of Essex.

Marco Baroni and Roberto Zamparelli. 2010. Nouns are vectors, adjectives are matrices: Representing adjective-noun constructions in semantic space. In *Proceedings of the 2010 Conference on Empirical Methods in Natural Language Processing,* East Stroudsburg, PA, pages 1183–1193.

Marco Baroni, Silvia Bernardini, Adriano Ferraresi, and Eros Zanchetta. 2009. The WaCky Wide Web: A Collection of Very Large Linguistically Processed Web-crawled Corpora. *Journal of Language Resources and Evaluation*, 43(3):209–226.

Marco Baroni, Brian Murphy, Eduard Barbu, and Massimo Poesio. 2010. Strudel. A Corpus-based Semantic Model based on Properties and Types. *Cognitive Science*, 34:222–254.

David M. Blei, Andrew Ng, and Michael Jordan. 2003. Latent Dirichlet Allocation. *JMLR*, 3:993–1022.

Asif Ekbal, Eva Sourjikova, Anette Frank, and Simone Ponzetto. 2010. Assessing the Challenge of Fine-grained Named Entity Recognition and Classification. In *Proceedings of the ACL 2010 Named Entity Workshop (NEWS)*, Uppsala, Sweden.

Christiane Fellbaum, editor. 1998. *WordNet: An Electronic Lexical Database*. MIT Press, Cambridge, Mass.

Emiliano Guevara. 2010. A regression model of adjective-noun compositionality in distributional semantics. In *Proceedings of the 2010 Workshop on GEometrical Models of Natural Language Semantics*, Stroudsburg, PA. Association for Computational Linguistics.

Matthias Hartung and Anette Frank. 2010. A Structured Vector Space Model for Hidden Attribute Meaning in Adjective-Noun Phrases. In *Proceedings of the 23rd International Conference on Computational Linguistics (COLING)*, Beijing, China, August.

Matthias Hartung and Anette Frank. 2011. Exploring Supervised LDA Models for Assigning Attributes to Adjective-Noun Phrases. In *Proceedings of the 2011 Conference on Empirical Methods in Natural Language Processing,* Edinburgh, UK.

Andrew Kachites McCallum. 2002. MALLET: A machine learning for language toolkit. http://mallet.cs.umass.edu.

Jeff Mitchell and Mirella Lapata. 2008. Vector-based Models of Semantic Composition. In *Proceedings of ACL-08: HLT*, pages 236–244, Columbus, Ohio, June.

Jeff Mitchell and Mirella Lapata. 2009. Language Models Based on Semantic Composition. In *Proceedings of the 2009 Conference on Empirical Methods in Natural Language Processing,* Singapore, August 2009, pages 430–439, Singapore, August.

Jeff Mitchell and Mirella Lapata. 2010. Composition in Distributional Models of Semantics. *Cognitive Science*, 34:1388–1429.

Diarmuid Ó Séaghdha. 2010. Latent variable models of selectional preference. In *Proceedings of the 48th Annual Meeting of the Association for Computational Linguistics*, pages 435–444, Uppsala, Sweden, July. Association for Computational Linguistics.

Alan Ritter, Mausam, and Oren Etzioni. 2010. A latent dirichlet allocation method for selectional preferences. In *Proceedings of the 48th Annual Meeting of the Association for Computational Linguistics*, pages 424–434, Uppsala, Sweden, July. Association for Computational Linguistics.

Peter D. Turney. 2008. A uniform approach to analogies, synonyms, antonyms, and associations. In *Proceedings of the 22nd International Conference on Computational Linguistics (Coling 2008)*, pages 905–912, Manchester, UK.

Experimenting with Transitive Verbs in a DisCoCat

Edward Grefenstette
University of Oxford
Department of Computer Science
Wolfson Building, Parks Road
Oxford OX1 3QD, UK
edward.grefenstette@cs.ox.ac.uk

Mehrnoosh Sadrzadeh
University of Oxford
Department of Computer Science
Wolfson Building, Parks Road
Oxford OX1 3QD, UK
mehrs@cs.ox.ac.uk

Abstract

Formal and distributional semantic models offer complementary benefits in modeling meaning. The categorical compositional distributional model of meaning of Coecke et al. (2010) (abbreviated to DisCoCat in the title) combines aspects of both to provide a general framework in which meanings of words, obtained distributionally, are composed using methods from the logical setting to form sentence meaning. Concrete consequences of this general abstract setting and applications to empirical data are under active study (Grefenstette et al., 2011; Grefenstette and Sadrzadeh, 2011). In this paper, we extend this study by examining transitive verbs, represented as matrices in a DisCoCat. We discuss three ways of constructing such matrices, and evaluate each method in a disambiguation task developed by Grefenstette and Sadrzadeh (2011).

1 Background

The categorical distributional compositional model of meaning of Coecke et al. (2010) combines the modularity of formal semantic models with the empirical nature of vector space models of lexical semantics. The meaning of a sentence is defined to be the application of its grammatical structure—represented in a type-logical model—to the kronecker product of the meanings of its words, as computed in a distributional model. The concrete and experimental consequences of this setting, and other models that aim to bring together the logical and distributional approaches, are active topics in current natural language semantics research, e.g. see (Grefenstette et al., 2011; Grefenstette and Sadrzadeh, 2011; Clark et al., 2010; Baroni and Zamparelli, 2010; Guevara, 2010; Mitchell and Lapata, 2008).

In this paper, we focus on our recent concrete DisCoCat model (Grefenstette and Sadrzadeh, 2011) and in particular on nouns composed with transitive verbs. Whereby the meaning of a transitive sentence 'sub tverb obj' is obtained by taking the component-wise multiplication of the matrix of the verb with the kronecker product of the vectors of subject and object:

$$\overrightarrow{\text{sub tverb obj}} = \underline{\text{tverb}} \odot (\overrightarrow{\text{sub}} \otimes \overrightarrow{\text{obj}}) \qquad (1)$$

In most logical models, transitive verbs are modeled as relations; in the categorical model the relational nature of such verbs gets manifested in their matrix representation: if subject and object are each r-dimensional row vectors in some space N, the verb will be a $r \times r$ matrix in the space $N \otimes N$. There are different ways of learning the weights of this matrix. In (Grefenstette and Sadrzadeh, 2011), we developed and implemented one such method on the data from the British National Corpus. The matrix of each verb was constructed by taking the sum of the kronecker products of all of the subject/object pairs linked to that verb in the corpus. We refer to this method as the *indirect method*. This is because the weight c_{ij} is obtained from the weights of the subject and object vectors (computed via co-occurrence with bases $\overrightarrow{n}_i$ and $\overrightarrow{n}_j$ respectively), rather than directly from the context of the verb itself, as would be the case in lexical distributional models. This construction method was evaluated against an extension of Mitchell and Lapata (2008)'s disambiguation task from intransitive to transitive sentences. We showed and discussed how and why our method, which is moreover scalable and respects the grammatical structure of the sentence, resulted in better results than other known models of semantic vector composition.

As a motivation for the current paper, note that there are at least two different factors at work in Equation (1): one is the matrix of the verb, denoted by $\underline{\text{tverb}}$, and the other is the kronecker product of subject and object vectors $\overrightarrow{\text{sub}} \otimes \overrightarrow{\text{obj}}$. Our model's mathematical formulation of composition prohibits us from changing the latter kronecker product, but the 'content' of the verb matrices can be built through different procedures.

In recent work we used a standard lexical distributional model for nouns and engineered our verbs to have a more sophisticated structure because of the higher dimensional space they occupy. In particular, we argued that the resulting matrix of the verb should represent 'the extent according to which the verb has related the properties of subjects to the properties of its objects', developed a general procedure to build such matrices, then studied their empirical consequences. One question remained open: what would be the consequence of starting from the standard lexical vector of the verb, then encoding it into the higher dimensional space using different (possibly ad-hoc but nonetheless interesting) mathematically inspired methods.

In a nutshell, the lexical vector of the verb is denoted by $\overrightarrow{\text{tverb}}$ and similar to vectors of subject and object, it is an r-dimensional row vector. Since the kronecker product of subject and object $(\overrightarrow{\text{sub}} \otimes \overrightarrow{\text{obj}})$ is $r \times r$, in order to make $\overrightarrow{\text{tverb}}$ applicable in Equation 1, i.e. to be able to substitute it for $\underline{\text{tverb}}$, we need to encode it into a $r \times r$ matrix in the $N \otimes N$ space. In what follows, we investigate the empirical consequences of three different encodings methods.

2 From Vectors to Matrices

In this section, we discuss three different ways of encoding r dimensional lexical verb vectors into $r \times r$ verb matrices, and present empirical results for each. We use the additional structure that the kronecker product provides to represent the relational nature of transitive verbs. The results are an indication that the extra information contained in this larger space contributes to higher quality composition.

One way to encode an r-dimensional vector as a $r \times r$ matrix is to embed it as the diagonal of that matrix. It remains open to decide what the non-diagonal values should be. We experimented with 0s and 1s as padding values. If the vector of the verb is $[c_1, c_2, \cdots, c_r]$ then for the 0 case (referred to as **0-diag**) we obtain the following matrix:

$$\underline{\text{tverb}} = \begin{pmatrix} c_1 & 0 & \cdots & 0 \\ 0 & c_2 & \cdots & 0 \\ \vdots & \vdots & \ddots & \vdots \\ 0 & 0 & \ldots & c_r \end{pmatrix}$$

For the 1 case (referred to as **1-diag**) we obtain the following matrix:

$$\underline{\text{tverb}} = \begin{pmatrix} c_1 & 1 & \cdots & 1 \\ 1 & c_2 & \cdots & 1 \\ \vdots & \vdots & \ddots & \vdots \\ 1 & 1 & \ldots & c_r \end{pmatrix}$$

We also considered a third case where the vector is encoded into a matrix by taking the kronecker product of the verb vector with itself:

$$\underline{\text{tverb}} = \overrightarrow{\text{tverb}} \otimes \overrightarrow{\text{tverb}}$$

So for $\overrightarrow{\text{tverb}} = [c_1, c_2, \cdots, c_r]$ we obtain the following matrix:

$$\underline{\text{tverb}} = \begin{pmatrix} c_1c_1 & c_1c_2 & \cdots & c_1c_r \\ c_2c_1 & c_2c_2 & \cdots & c_2c_r \\ \vdots & \vdots & \ddots & \vdots \\ c_rc_1 & c_rc_2 & \cdots & c_rc_r \end{pmatrix}$$

3 Degrees of synonymity for sentences

The degree of synonymity between meanings of two sentences is computed by measuring their geometric distance. In this work, we used the cosine measure. For two sentences '$\text{sub}_1\ \text{tverb}_1\ \text{obj}_1$' and '$\text{sub}_2\ \text{tverb}_2\ \text{obj}_2$', this is obtained by taking the *Frobenius* inner product of $\overrightarrow{\text{sub}_1\ \text{tverb}_1\ \text{obj}_1}$ and $\overrightarrow{\text{sub}_2\ \text{tverb}_2\ \text{obj}_2}$. The use of *Frobenius* product rather than the dot product is because the calculation in Equation (1) produces matrices rather than row vectors. We normalized the outputs by the multiplication of the lengths of their corresponding matrices.

4 Experiment

In this section, we describe the experiment used to evaluate and compare these three methods. The experiment is on the dataset developed in (Grefenstette and Sadrzadeh, 2011).

Parameters We used the parameters described by Mitchell and Lapata (2008) for the noun and verb vectors. All vectors were built from a lemmatised version of the BNC. The noun basis was the 2000 most common context words, basis weights were the probability of context words given the target word divided by the overall probability of the context word. These features were chosen to enable easy comparison of our experimental results with those of Mitchell and Lapata's original experiment, in spite of the fact that there may be more sophisticated lexical distributional models available.

Task This is an extension of Mitchell and Lapata (2008)'s disambiguation task from intransitive to transitive sentences. The general idea behind the transitive case (similar to the intransitive one) is as follows: meanings of ambiguous transitive verbs vary based on their subject-object context. For instance the verb 'meet' means 'satisfied' in the context 'the system met the criterion' and it means 'visit', in the context 'the child met the house'. Hence if we build meaning vectors for these sentences compositionally, the degrees of synonymity of the sentences can be used to disambiguate the meanings of the verbs in them.

Suppose a verb has two meanings a and b and that it has occurred in two sentences. Then if in both of these sentences it has its meaning a, the two sentences will have a high degree of synonymity, whereas if in one sentence the verb has meaning a and in the other meaning b, the sentences will have a lower degree of synonymity. For instance 'the system met the criterion' and 'the system satisfied the criterion' have a high degree of semantic similarity, and similarly for 'the child met the house' and 'the child visited the house'. This degree decreases for the pair 'the child met the house' and 'the child satisfied the house'.

Dataset The dataset is built using the same guidelines as Mitchell and Lapata (2008), using transitive verbs obtained from CELEX[1] paired with subjects and objects. We first picked 10 transitive verbs from the most frequent verbs of the BNC. For each verb, two different non-overlapping meanings were retrieved, by using the JCN (Jiang Conrath) information content synonymity measure of WordNet to select maximally different synsets. For instance for 'meet' we obtained 'visit' and 'satisfy'. For each original verb, ten sentences containing that verb with the same role were retrieved from the BNC. Examples of such sentences are 'the system met the criterion' and 'the child met the house'. For each such sentence, we generated two other related sentences by substituting their verbs by each of their two synonyms. For instance, we obtained 'the system satisfied the criterion' and 'the system visited the criterion' for the first meaning and 'the child satisfied the house' and 'the child visited the house' for the second meaning . This procedure provided us with 200 pairs of sentences.

The dataset was split into four non-identical sections of 100 entries such that each sentence appears in exactly two sections. Each section was given to a group of evaluators who were asked to assign a similarity score to simple transitive sentence pairs formed from the verb, subject, and object provided in each entry (*e.g.* 'the system met the criterion' from 'system meet criterion'). The scoring scale for human judgement was $[1, 7]$, where 1 was most dissimilar and 7 most identical.

Separately from the group annotation, each pair in the dataset was given the additional arbitrary classification of HIGH or LOW similarity by the authors.

Evaluation Method To evaluate our methods, we first applied our formulae to compute the similarity of each phrase pair on a scale of $[0, 1]$ and then compared it with human judgement of the same pair. The comparison was performed by measuring Spearman's ρ, a rank correlation coefficient ranging from -1 to 1. This provided us with the degree of correlation between the similarities as computed by our model and as judged by human evaluators.

Following Mitchell and Lapata (2008), we also computed the mean of HIGH and LOW scores. However, these scores were solely based on the authors' personal judgements and as such (and on their

[1]http://celex.mpi.nl/

own) do not provide a very reliable measure. Therefore, like Mitchell and Lapata (2008), the models were ultimately judged by Spearman's ρ.

The results are presented in table 4. The additive and multiplicative rows have, as composition operation, vector addition and component-wise multiplication. The *Baseline* is from a non-compositional approach; it is obtained by comparing the verb vectors of each pair directly and ignoring their subjects and objects. The *UpperBound* is set to be inter-annotator agreement.

Model	High	Low	ρ
Baseline	0.47	0.44	0.16
Add	0.90	0.90	0.05
Multiply	0.67	0.59	0.17
Categorical			
Indirect matrix	**0.73**	**0.72**	**0.21**
0-diag matrix	**0.67**	**0.59**	**0.17**
1-diag matrix	**0.86**	**0.85**	**0.08**
$v \otimes v$ **matrix**	**0.34**	**0.26**	**0.28**
UpperBound	4.80	2.49	0.62

Table 1: Results of compositional disambiguation.

The **indirect matrix** performed better than the vectors encoded in diagonal matrices padded with 0 and 1. However, surprisingly, the kronecker product of this vector with itself provided better results than all the above. The results were statistically significant with $p < 0.05$.

5 Analysis of the Results

Suppose the vector of $\underline{\text{subject}}$ is $[s_1, s_2, \cdots, s_r]$ and the vector of $\underline{\text{object}}$ is $\overrightarrow{\text{obj}} = [o_1, o_2, \cdots, o_r]$, then the matrix of $\overrightarrow{\text{sub}} \otimes \overrightarrow{\text{obj}}$ is:

$$\begin{pmatrix} s_1o_1 & s_1o_2 & \cdots & s_1o_r \\ s_2o_1 & s_2o_2 & \cdots & s_2o_r \\ \vdots & & & \\ s_ro_1 & s_ro_2 & \cdots & s_ro_r \end{pmatrix}$$

After computing Equation (1) for each generation method of $\underline{\text{tverb}}$, we obtain the following three matrices for the meaning of a transitive sentence:

$$\textbf{0-diag}: \begin{pmatrix} c_1s_1o_1 & 0 & \cdots & 0 \\ 0 & c_2s_2o_2 & \cdots & 0 \\ \vdots & \vdots & \ddots & \vdots \\ 0 & 0 & \cdots & c_rs_ro_r \end{pmatrix}$$

This method discards all of the non-diagonal information about the subject and object, for example there is no occurrence of s_1o_2, s_2o_1, etc.

$$\textbf{1-diag}: \begin{pmatrix} c_1s_1o_1 & s_1o_2 & \cdots & s_1o_r \\ s_2o_1 & c_2s_2o_2 & \cdots & s_2o_r \\ \vdots & \vdots & \ddots & \vdots \\ s_ro_1 & s_ro_2 & \cdots & c_rs_ro_r \end{pmatrix}$$

This method conserves the information about the subject and object, but only applies the information of the verb to the diagonals: s_1 and o_2, s_2 and o_1, etc. are never related to each other via the verb.

$$v \otimes v: \begin{pmatrix} c_1c_1s_1o_1 & c_1c_2s_1o_2 & \cdots & c_1c_rs_1o_r \\ c_2c_1s_2o_1 & c_2c_2s_2o_2 & \cdots & c_2c_rs_2o_r \\ \vdots & \vdots & \ddots & \vdots \\ c_rc_1s_ro_1 & c_rc_2s_ro_2 & \cdots & c_rc_rs_ro_r \end{pmatrix}$$

This method not only conserves the information of the subject and object, but also applies to them all of the information encoded in the verb. These data propagate to *Frobenius* products when computing the semantic similarity of sentences and justify the empirical results.

The unexpectedly good performance of the $v \otimes v$ matrix relative to the more complex indirect method is surprising, and certainly demands further investigation. What is sure is that they each draw upon different aspects of semantic composition to provide better results. There is certainly room for improvement and empirical optimisation in both of these relation-matrix construction methods.

Furthermore, the success of both of these methods relative to the others examined in Table 1 shows that it is the extra information provided in the matrix (rather than just the diagonal, representing the lexical vector) that encodes the *relational nature* of transitive verbs, thereby validating in part the requirement suggested in Coecke et al. (2010) and Grefenstette and Sadrzadeh (2011) that relational word vectors live in a space the dimensionality of which be a function of the arity of the relation.

References

H. Alshawi (ed). 1992. *The Core Language Engine*. MIT Press.

M. Baroni and R. Zamparelli. 2010. *Nouns are vectors, adjectives are matrices*. Proceedings of Conference on Empirical Methods in Natural Language Processing (EMNLP).

D. Clarke, R. Lutz and D. Weir. 2010. *Semantic Composition with Quotient Algebras*. Proceedings of Geometric Models of Natural Language Semantics (GEMS-2010).

S. Clark and S. Pulman. 2007. *Combining Symbolic and Distributional Models of Meaning*. Proceedings of AAAI Spring Symposium on Quantum Interaction. AAAI Press.

B. Coecke, M. Sadrzadeh and S. Clark. 2010. *Mathematical Foundations for Distributed Compositional Model of Meaning*. Lambek Festschrift. Linguistic Analysis **36**, 345–384. J. van Benthem, M. Moortgat and W. Buszkowski (eds.).

J. Curran. 2004. *From Distributional to Semantic Similarity*. PhD Thesis, University of Edinburgh.

K. Erk and S. Padó. 2004. *A Structured Vector Space Model for Word Meaning in Context*. Proceedings of Conference on Empirical Methods in Natural Language Processing (EMNLP), 897–906.

G. Frege 1892. *Über Sinn und Bedeutung*. Zeitschrift für Philosophie und philosophische Kritik 100.

J. R. Firth. 1957. *A synopsis of linguistic theory 1930-1955*. Studies in Linguistic Analysis.

E. Grefenstette, M. Sadrzadeh, S. Clark, B. Coecke, S. Pulman. 2011. *Concrete Compositional Sentence Spaces for a Compositional Distributional Model of Meaning*. International Conference on Computational Semantics (IWCS'11). Oxford.

E. Grefenstette, M. Sadrzadeh. 2011. *Experimental Support for a Categorical Compositional Distributional Model of Meaning*. Proceedings of the 2011 Conference on Empirical Methods in Natural Language Processing.

G. Grefenstette. 1994. *Explorations in Automatic Thesaurus Discovery*. Kluwer.

E. Guevara. 2010. *A Regression Model of Adjective-Noun Compositionality in Distributional Semantics*. Proceedings of the ACL GEMS Workshop.

Z. S. Harris. 1966. *A Cycling Cancellation-Automaton for Sentence Well-Formedness*. International Computation Centre Bulletin **5**, 69–94.

R. Hudson. 1984. *Word Grammar*. Blackwell.

J. Lambek. 2008. *From Word to Sentence*. Polimetrica, Milan.

T. Landauer, and S. Dumais. 2008. *A solution to Platos problem: The latent semantic analysis theory of acquisition, induction, and representation of knowledge*. Psychological review.

C. D. Manning, P. Raghavan, and H. Schütze. 2008. *Introduction to information retrieval*. Cambridge University Press.

J. Mitchell and M. Lapata. 2008. *Vector-based models of semantic composition*. Proceedings of the 46th Annual Meeting of the Association for Computational Linguistics, 236–244.

R. Montague. 1974. *English as a formal language*. Formal Philosophy, 189–223.

J. Nivre 2003. *An efficient algorithm for projective dependency parsing*. Proceedings of the 8th International Workshop on Parsing Technologies (IWPT).

J. Saffron, E. Newport, R. Asling. 1999. *Word Segmentation: The role of distributional cues*. Journal of Memory and Language **35**, 606–621.

H. Schuetze. 1998. *Automatic Word Sense Discrimination*. Computational Linguistics **24**, 97–123.

P. Smolensky. 1990. *Tensor product variable binding and the representation of symbolic structures in connectionist systems*. Computational Linguistics **46, 1–2**, 159–216.

M. Steedman. 2000. *The Syntactic Process*. MIT Press.

D. Widdows. 2005. *Geometry and Meaning*. University of Chicago Press.

L. Wittgenstein. 1953. *Philosophical Investigations*. Blackwell.

A distributional similarity approach to the detection of semantic change in the Google Books Ngram corpus

Kristina Gulordava
DISI, University of Trento
Trento, Italy
kgulordava@gmail.com

Marco Baroni
CIMeC, University of Trento
Trento, Italy
marco.baroni@unitn.it

Abstract

This paper presents a novel approach for automatic detection of semantic change of words based on distributional similarity models. We show that the method obtains good results with respect to a reference ranking produced by human raters. The evaluation also analyzes the performance of frequency-based methods, comparing them to the similarity method proposed.

1 Introduction

Recently a large corpus of digitized books was made publicly available by Google (Mitchel et al., 2010). It contains more than 5 millions of books published between the sixteenth century and today. Computational analysis of such representative diachronic data made it possible to trace different cultural trends in the last centuries. Mitchel et al. (2010) exploit the change in word frequency as the main measure for the quantitative investigation of cultural and linguistic phenomena; in this paper, we extend this approach by measuring the semantic similarity of the word occurrences in two different time points using *distributional semantics model* (Turney and Pantel, 2010).

Semantic change, defined as a change of one or more meanings of the word in time (Lehmann, 1992), is of interest to historical linguistics and is related to the natural language processing task of unknown word sense detection (Erk, 2006). Developing automatic methods for identifying changes in word meaning can therefore be useful for both theoretical linguistics and a variety of NLP applications which depend on lexical information.

Some first automatic approaches to the semantic change detection task were recently proposed by Sagi et al. (2009) and Cook and Stevenson (2010). These works focus on specific types of semantic change, i.e., Sagi et al. (2009) aim to identify widening and narrowing of meaning, while Cook and Stevenson (2010) concentrate on amelioration and pejoration cases. Their evaluation of the proposed methods is rather qualitative, concerning just a few examples.

In present work we address the task of automatic detection of the semantic change of words in quantitative way, comparing our novel distributional similarity approach to a relative-frequency-based method. For the evaluation, we used the Google Books Ngram data from the 1960s and 1990s, taking as a reference standard a ranking produced by human raters. We present the results of the method proposed, which highly correlate with the human judgements on a test set, and show the underlying relations with relative frequency.

2 Google Books Ngram corpus

The overall data published online by Google represent a collection of digitized books with over 500 billion words in 7 different languages distributed in n-gram format due to copyright limitations (Mitchel et al., 2010). An n-gram is a sequence of n words divided by space character; for each n-gram it is specified in which year it occurred and how many times.

For our diachronic investigation we used the American English 2-grams corpus (with over 150 millions 2-grams) and extracted two time slices from the 1960s and 1990s time periods. More precisely, we automatically selected 2-grams with year of occurrence between 1960 and 1964 for the 1960s slice, and between 1995 and 1999 for the 1990s slice, and summed up the number of occurrences of each 2-gram for both corpora. After preprocessing, we obtained well-balanced 60s and 90s corpora containing around 25 and 28 millions of 2-grams, respectively.

We consider the 60s and 90s to be interesting time frames for the evaluation, having in mind that a lot of words underwent semantic change between these decades due to many significant technological and social movements. At the same time, the 60s are close enough so that non-experts should have good intuitions about semantic change between then and now, which, in turn, makes it possible to collect reference judgments from human raters.

3 Measuring semantic change

3.1 Relative frequency

Many previous diachronic studies in corpus linguistics focused on changes of relative frequency of the words to detect different kinds of phenomena (Hilpert and Gries, 2009; Mitchel et al., 2010). Intuitively, such approach can also be applied to detect semantic change, as one would expect that many words that are more popular nowadays with respect to the past (in our case: the 60s) have changed their meaning or gained an alternative one. Semantic change could explain a significant growth of the relative frequency of the word.

Therefore we decided to take as a competing measure for evaluation the logarithmic ratio between frequency of word occurrence in the 60s and frequency of word occurrence in the 90s[1].

3.2 Distributional similarity

In the distributional semantics approach (see for example Turney and Pantel, 2010), the similarity between words can be quantified by how frequently they appear within the same context in large corpora. These distributional properties of the words are described by a vector space model where each word is associated with its context vector. The way a context is defined can vary in different applications. The one we use here is the most common approach which considers contexts of a word as a set of all other words with which it co-occurs. In our case we decided to use 2-grams, that is, only words that occur right next to the given word are considered as part of its context. The window of length 2 was chosen for practical reasons given the huge size or the Google Ngram corpus, but it has been shown to produce good results in previous studies (e.g. Bullinaria and Levy, 2007). The words and their context vectors create a so called co-occurrence matrix, where row elements are target words and column elements are context terms.

The scores of the constructed co-occurrence matrix are given by local mutual information (LMI) scores (Evert, 2008) computed on the frequency counts of corresponding 2-grams[2]. If words w_1 and w_2 occurred $C(w_1, w_2)$ times together and $C(w_1)$ and $C(w_2)$ times overall in corpus then local mutual information score is defined as follows:

$$LMI = C(w_1, w_2) \cdot \log_2 \frac{C(w_1, w_2)N}{C(w_1)C(w_2)},$$

where N is the overall number of 2-gram in the corpus.

Given the words w_1, w_2 their distributional similarity is then measured as the cosine product of their context vectors $\mathbf{v}_1, \mathbf{v}_2$: $sim(w_1, w_2) = \cos(\mathbf{v}_1, \mathbf{v}_2)$.

We apply this model to measure similarity of a word occurrences in two corpora of different time periods in the following way. The set of context elements is fixed and remains the same for both corpora; for each corpus, a context vector for a word is extracted independently, using counts in this corpus as discussed above. In this way, each word will have a 60s vector and a 90s vector, with the same dimensions (context elements), but different co-occurrence counts. The vectors can be compared by computing the cosine of their angle. Since the context vectors are computed in the same vector space, the procedure is completely equivalent to calculating similarity between two different words in the same corpora; the context vectors can be considered as belonging to one co-occurrence matrix and corresponding to two different row elements $word\_60s$ and $word\_90s$.

[1] The logarithmic ratio helps intuition (terms more popular in the 60s get negative scores, terms more popular in the 90s have similarly scaled positive scores), but omitting the logarithmic transform produced similar results in evaluation.

[2] LMI proved to be a good measure for different semantic tasks, see for example the work of Baroni and Lenci, 2010.

group	examples	sim	freq
more frequent in 90s	users	0.29	-0.94
	sleep	0.23	-0.32
	disease	0.87	-0.3
	card	0.17	-0.1
more frequent in 60s	dealers	0.16	0.04
	coach	0.25	0.12
	energy	0.79	0.14
	cent	0.99	1.13

Table 1: Examples illustrating word selection with similarity (sim) and log-frequency (freq) metric values.

	sim-HR	freq-HR	sim-freq
all words	**0.386****	0.301**	0.380**
frequent in 90s	0.445**	0.184	0.278*
frequent in 60s	0.163	0.310	0.406*

Table 2: Correlation between similarity (sim), frequency (freq) and human ranking (HR) values for all words, words more frequent in 60s and more frequent in 90s. Values statistically significant for $p = 0.01(0.05)$ in one-sample t-test are marked with **(*).

We use the described procedure to measure semantic change of a word in two corpora of interest, and hence between two time periods. High similarity value (close to 1) would suggest that a word has not undergone semantic change, while obtaining low similarity (close to 0) should indicate a noticeable change in the meaning and the use of the word.

4 Experiments

4.1 Distributional space construction

To be able to compute distributional similarity for the words in the 60s and 90s corpora, we randomly chose 250,000 mid-frequency words as the context elements of the vector space. We calculated 60s-to-90s similarity values for a list of 10,000 randomly picked mid-frequency words. Among these words, 48.4% had very high similarity values (> 0.8), 50% average similarity (from 0.2 to 0.8) and only 1.6% had very low similarity (< 0.2). According to our prediction, this last group of words would be the ones that underwent semantic change.

To test such hypothesis in a quantitative way some reference standard must be available. Since for our task there was no appropriate database containing words classified for semantic change, we decided to create a reference categorization using human judgements.

4.2 Human evaluation

From the list of 10,000 words we chose 100 as a representative random subset containing words with different similarities from the whole scale from 0 to 1 and taken from different frequency range, i.e., words that became more frequent in 90s (60%) and words that became less frequent (40%) (see Table 1 for examples). Human raters were asked to rank the resulting list according to their intuitions about change in last 40 years on a 4-point scale (0: no change; 1: almost no change; 2: somewhat change; 3: changed significantly). We took the average of judgments as the reference value with which distributional similarity scores were compared. For the 5 participants, the inter-rater agreement, computed as an average of pair-wise Pearson correlations, was 0.51 ($p < 0.01$). It shows that the collected judgements were highly correlated and the average judgement can be considered an enough reliable reference for semantic change measurements evaluation.

5 Results and discussion

To assess the performance of our similarity-based measure, we computed the correlations between the values it produced for our list of words and the average human judgements (Table 2). The Pearson correlation value obtained was equal to 0.38, which is reasonably high given 0.51 inter-rater agreement. The frequency measure had a lower correlation (0.3), though close to the similarity measure performance. Yet, the correlation of 0.38 between the two measures in question suggests that, even if they perform similarly, their predictions could be quite different.

In fact, if we consider separately two groups of words: the ones whose frequency increased in the 90s (*log-freq* < 0), that is, the ones that are more popular nowadays, and those whose frequency instead decreased in the 90s (*log-freq* > 0), that is, the ones that were more popular in the 60s, we can make some interesting observations (see Table 2). Remarkably, similarity performs better for the words that are popular nowadays while the frequency-based measure performs better for the words that were popular in the 60s.

We can see the origin of this peculiar asymmetry in behavior of similarity and frequency measures in the following phenomenon. As we already mentioned, if a word became popular, the reason can be a new sense it acquired (a lot of technological terms are of this kind: *'disk'*, *'address'*, etc). The change in such words, that are characterized by a significant growth in frequency (*log-freq* $\ll 0$), is detected by the human judges, as well as by the similarity measure. However, other cases such as *'spine'*, *'smoking'* are also characterized by a significant growth in frequency, but no semantic change was reported by raters (nor by the similarity measure). If word frequency instead decreases, intuitively, a change in word meaning is less probable. These intuitions together can explain the behavior of the frequency measure: for the test set as a whole its performance is quite high, as it captures this asymmetrical distribution of words that change meanings, despite its failure to reliably indicate semantic change for independent words. A strong evidence for this interpretation is also that, if the frequency measure is made symmetric, that is, equal for the words that decreased and the ones that increased in frequency, it dramatically drops in performance, showing a correlation of just 0.04 with human ranking.

Some interesting observation regarding the performance of the similarity measure can be made after accurate investigation of 'false-positive' examples — the ones that have low similarity but were ranked as 'not changed' by raters — like *'sleep'* and *'parent'*. It is enough to have a look at their highest weighted co-occurrences to admit that the context of their usage has indeed changed (Table 3). These examples show the difference between the phenomenon of semantic change in linguistics and the case of context change. It is well known that the different contexts that distributional semantics catches do not always directly refer to what linguists would consider distinct senses (Reisinger and Mooney, 2010). Most people would agree that the word *'parent'* has the same meaning now as it had 40 years before, still the social context in which it is used has evidently changed, reflected by the more frequent *'single parent family(ies)'* collocate found in the 90s. The same is true for *'sleep'*, whose usage context did not change radically, but might have a more prominent negative orientation.

	'parent'	'sleep'
60s	p. company 2643	deep s. 3803
	p. education 1905	s. well 1403
	p. corporation 1617	cannot s. 1124
	p. material 1337	long s. 1102
	p. body 1082	sound s. 1101
	p. compound 818	dreamless s. 844
	common p. 816	much s. 770
90s	p. families 17710	REM s. 20150
	single p. 10724	s. apnea 14768
	p. company 8367	deep s. 8482
	p. education 5884	s. disorders 8427
	p. training 5847	s. deprivation 6108
	p. involvement 5591	s. disturbances 5973
	p. family 5042	s. disturbance 5251

Table 3: Examples of the top weighted 2-grams containing 'sleep' and 'parent'.

The distributional similarity measure captures therefore two kinds of phenomena: the semantic change in its linguistic definition, that is, change of meaning or acquiring a new sense (e.g., *'virus'*, *'virtual'*), but also the change in the main context in which the word is used. The latter, in turn, can be an important preliminary evidence of the onset of meaning change in its traditional sense, according to recent studies on language change (Traugott and Dasher, 2002). Moreover, context changes have cultural and social origins, and therefore the similarity measure can also be used for collecting evidence of interest to the humanities and social sciences.

6 Conclusions

In this paper we introduced and evaluated a novel automatic approach for measuring semantic change with a distributional similarity model. The similarity-based measure produces good results, obtaining high correlation with human judgements on test data. The study also suggests that the method can be suitable to detect both "proper" semantic change of words, and cases of major diachronic context change. Therefore, it can be useful for historical linguistic studies as well as for NLP tasks such as novel sense detection. Some interesting phenomena related to changes in relative frequency were also discovered, and will be the object of further investigations.

References

Marco Baroni, Alessandro Lenci. 2010. Distributional memory: A general framework for corpus-based semantics. *Computational Linguistics*, 36(4):673–721. MIT Press, Cambridge, MA, USA.

John A. Bullinaria, Joseph P. Levy. 2007. Extracting Semantic Representations from Word Co-occurrence Statistics: A Computational Study. *Behavior Research Methods*, 39: 510-526.

Paul Cook, Suzanne Stevenson. 2010. Automatically identifying changes in the semantic orientation of words. *Proceedings of the 7th International Conference on Language Resources and Evaluation.* Valletta, Malta: 28–34.

Katrin Erk. 2006. Unknown word sense detection as outlier detection. *Proceedings of the Human Language Technology of the North American Chapter of the ACL.* New York, USA: 128–135.

Stefan Evert. 2008. Corpora and collocations. In A. Ldeling and M. Kyt (eds.), *Corpus Linguistics. An International Handbook*, article 58. Mouton de Gruyter, Berlin.

Hilpert Martin, Stefan Th. Gries. 2009. Assessing frequency changes in multi-stage diachronic corpora: applications for historical corpus linguistics and the study of language acquisition. *Literary and Linguistic Computing*, 34(4): 385-40.

Winfred P. Lehmann. 1992. *Historical linguistics: an introduction.* (3. ed.) Routledge & Kegan Paul, London.

Jean-Baptiste Michel*, Yuan Kui Shen, Aviva Presser Aiden, Adrian Veres, Matthew K. Gray, William Brockman, The Google Books Team, Joseph P. Pickett, Dale Hoiberg, Dan Clancy, Peter Norvig, Jon Orwant, Steven Pinker, Martin A. Nowak, and Erez Lieberman Aiden*. 2010. Quantitative Analysis of Culture Using Millions of Digitized Books. *Science* (Published online ahead of print: 12/16/2010).

Joseph Reisinger, Raymond Mooney. 2010. A Mixture Model with Sharing for Lexical Semantics. *Proceedings of the Conference on Empirical Methods in Natural Language Processing.* MIT, Massachusetts, USA: 1173–1182.

Eyal Sagi, Stefan Kaufmann, Brady Clark. 2009. Semantic Density Analysis: Comparing Word Meaning across Time and Phonetic Space. *Proceedings of the EACL 2009 Workshop on GEMS: Geometrical Models of Natural Language Semantics.* Athens, Greece: 104–111.

Elizabeth C. Traugott, Richard B. Dasher. 2002. *Regularity in Semantic Change.* Cambridge University Press.

Peter Turney, Patrick Pantel. 2010. From Frequency to Meaning: Vector Space Models of Semantics. *Journal of Artificial Intelligence Research (JAIR)*, 37(1):141-188. AI Access Foundation.

Author Index

Association for Computational Linguistics
209 N. Eighth Street
Stroudsburg, Pennsylvania 18360